Cry With Me: Part 1

Aida wearing her great-grandmother's best hat

Cry With Me: Part 1

The True Story About a Woman from Africa Seeking Asylum in Britain

Mabel Ann Pike

iUniverse, Inc.
New York Lincoln Shanghai

Cry With Me: Part 1
The True Story About a Woman from Africa Seeking Asylum in Britain

iUniverse books may be ordered through booksellers or by contacting:

iUniverse
2021 Pine Lake Road, Suite 100
Lincoln, NE 68512
www.iuniverse.com
1-800-Authors (1-800-288-4677)

ISBN-13: 978-0-595-41167-2 (pbk)
ISBN-13: 978-0-595-67874-7 (cloth)
ISBN-13: 978-0-595-85524-7 (ebk)
ISBN-10: 0-595-41167-3 (pbk)
ISBN-10: 0-595-67874-2 (cloth)
ISBN-10: 0-595-85524-5 (ebk)

Printed in the United States of America

This book is dedicated to

The loving memory of my beautiful and wonderful daughter Aida Ann Jenkins (1973–1987) who showed me the meaning of true love and who every day brought sunshine into my life.

The many 'angels', both Muslim and Christian, who came to my assistance in my hour of need and asked for nothing in return.

Elizabeth the Second, by the Grace of God, of the United Kingdom and Northern Island and her other Realms and Territories, Queen, Head of the Commonwealth, Defender of the Faith.

Contents

Acknowledgements

I am indebted to the following for their kind assistance:

Bernice Walmsley for her assistance in writing the book;
Mrs Sylvia Eccles for translating details of Aida's medical condition into plain English;
The Internet for helping me find details of place names, hospitals, schools, etc.

Foreword

It is not often that one gets the chance to relive the real horrors that asylum seekers face when fleeing their countries for a safe haven. Quite often the real story gets lost in the midst of media and government propaganda related to bogus asylum seekers. *Cry With Me* is a fascinating and heart wrenching account of one woman's struggles through the horrors unleashed by Mugabe's regime in Zimbabwe against innocent victims due to their skin colour. Throughout her account Mabel Pike shines through as a brave mother whose only wish was to have a safe, respectful and happy life without fear for her life just because of her skin colour.

—*Aisha Latif*
(The author's solicitor.)

Preface

Cry With Me is an asylum seeker's account of courage and perseverance. It tells how for years the author suffered the indignities, humiliations and anguish of racial prejudice and violence in Zimbabwe with its eroding economy and disintegrating law and order, finally seeking refuge in Britain, the home of her grandfather.

Mabel's story, well told and a page-turner in itself, is a moving and heartrending, personal account about how she grew up and suffered untold hardships and injustices in a war-torn and corrupt African country—Zimbabwe—and how she finally took the courageous step to seek asylum in Britain. Mabel, who writes from the heart, recreates the loving relationship she had as a child with her Shona grandmother, a practical woman who, though married to a white British man, lived simply, preferring to sleep on the floor by the stove and eat her bush meals than live by western standards. The warm, loving relationship with her family, her parents and her children, shine through the various tragedies and hardships. She is ruthlessly honest in describing the inhuman cruelties of the guerrillas ('freedom fighters' or 'war veterans') who murdered and raped her cousin, plundered her father's farms, and the Zimbabwean police who 'arrested' and abused her, throwing her into a stinking prison without clothes when she was nine months pregnant. The ultimate poignancy comes from the anguish with which she recreates her sweet daughter Aida's plight, dying from a kidney infection in the unhygienic and appallingly filthy conditions of hospitals in Zimbabwe. Though Mabel proved herself to be an enterprising and resourceful businesswoman, the persistent harassment of government officials, the unrelenting havoc of crime and plunder, eventually drove her to seek a new life in Britain, the home of her forefathers. However, the five-year long and ongoing delay in granting her asylum, with the prospect of her being returned to the Zimbabwe hell-hole at the age of 53, has constituted a veritable sword of Damocles hanging over her life, resulting in stress and ill-health.

The inspiring flame that lights up this book of sorrow and challenge is unfading hope, which Mabel has kept alive throughout her life. Mabel, a committed disciple of Jesus, never abandons hope; and the love, the grace, that her faith engenders brings home to us the message that there is always a light at the end of the tunnel—and, indeed, the book ends on an upbeat note with new prospects ahead. Mabel has proved herself to be a woman of faith; without it she would not be where she is now, and would not be the sweet person she is; indeed, without this sustaining hope she would not have survived the long journey that has brought her to Britain. As we are told in Hebrews, faith is the substance of things hoped for, the evidence of things unseen. As Mabel says at the end of this book, she hopes that the people who read her story, which is a true story, will start believing in caring for one another and not think that everyone who seeks asylum is bad. Seeking asylum, she says, is a big move: "It means starting again from the beginning and escaping from a bad life." And that takes courage as well as hope.

Charles Muller, MA (Wales), PhD (Lond), DLitt (OFS), DEd (SA)
Diadem Books

More information at ***www.diadembooks.com/asylum.htm***

1

My beginnings

In a small, deserted town, far away from the rest of the world, I was born. I was delivered by my father's elder sister, Esther, who came all the way from Salisbury, the capital city. Nowadays Salisbury is called Harare and it was about four hundred and fifty miles away from the remote town where I started my life. Esther was the midwife even though she had no formal experience of delivering a baby. My parents could not afford to go to the hospital or get a trained midwife to help so she stepped in to help with the birth. That's why to this day she still calls me her special baby. It was a smooth delivery and on the 26th of December 1952, the day after Christmas, I made my entry into the world.

My name is Mabel. I am from Zimbabwe in Africa but at the time I was born it was a beautiful British Colony called Southern Rhodesia (which became simply Rhodesia after 1965) and was ruled by the white minority. I grew up in a small town called Selukwe, which is now known as Shurugwi. It is a small, mountainous town with breathtaking scenery. As far as you can see there is a patchwork of green fields. The fertile soil of the area means that there are farms growing all sorts of crops. There were only a handful of people living in Selukwe during my childhood and they all relied, in some form or another, on the crops grown on the farms. In those days it was a truly beautiful place to live and was a peaceful, almost sleepy existence but lots of things were to change when Rhodesia became Zimbabwe.

It was decided that after I was born my mother's parents would look after me. My mother was barely sixteen, my father was seventeen and both they and their families felt that they were too young to have the responsibilities of looking after a child. They were also keen to make a good start in life for themselves in the big city of Salisbury where they could get good jobs and build a future for their new family. Their being so far away meant that I would rarely see my parents during my childhood, but this was quite common in our society.

Mother and me

My Grandfather, known by friends as Jimmy, came to Southern Rhodesia from Blackheath, Surrey, in Britain, in the 1930's with his younger brother, Charley. Both of them were white British. My grandfather was well off when he came to Rhodesia and bought a very big farm. This was called Marrow Farm, which was next door to Gwenara Farm which was later acquired by Ian Smith, the future prime minister of Rhodesia. He had more than a thousand acres of land, where he raised herds of cattle and sheep and also started up little shops. He hired men to sit on the verandas, working hard in the shade with sewing machines, busily making clothes for all the people in the surrounding areas. Grandfather also grew vegetables and fields of maize that seemed to go on and on forever. His business interests were wide-ranging and he owned a mill, open for twenty-four hours a day, which used to grind the maize that had grown in his fields into a powder. The local people bought this maize powder to cook the local speciality called *sadza*. I remember that my grandfather, for some reason, called this 'pup'.

My grandfather showed the local people nothing but kindness and he was loved by all the people who knew him. He always tried to help where he could, providing the poor people with food and clothing. As a family we had lots of respect from our surrounding neighbours—most of them thought my grandfather was an angel sent by God. I have a vivid memory of him with his big baggy grey trousers kept in place by some braces, worn with a very clean white shirt tucked neatly into his trousers. He wore farmer's shoes. This was how he would dress every day except Sunday when he wore his best shoes and his little round grey hat.

My Father

My grandmother was a black African woman named Jessie. She never spoke a word of English—only her native language Shona. I sometimes wonder how she and my grandfather managed to communicate. They obviously got by very well because he showed her the greatest respect and admiration. She was plain and simple in many ways but had very strong beliefs and was set in her ways. She was brought up to believe that ancestor worship was a way of life. Obedience to your elders is absolute and unquestioned and to rebel against the word of your elders is to invite social censure of enormous magnitude. Women are at the very bottom of the ladder and exist merely to obey and serve men and to give birth to male children. She always wore long black skirts with black or brown tops and all her clothes were always oversized, with about two or three petticoats worn under them. I will never understand why she dressed like this. Her hair was always hidden under a scarf or hat, even when she was sleeping, so I never knew what colour it was or how her hair looked. I often used to wonder whether it was plaited or not, but that was a little secret of hers. Occasionally you would see her in tennis shoes, but most of the time she would be barefooted, even when she was out working in the fields. Just like my grandfather, my grandmother had her 'Sunday best'. To church she always wore a nice pair of shiny black leather shoes.

My grandmother was a very hard working lady. She got up first thing in the morning—at five o'clock, when it was still dark—and immediately made a fire to boil water for our tea. Then she would make sure the yard was clean by sweeping right around the sprawling house, using a large stick with green leaves tied to it to make a broom. All this would be done before six o'clock each morning. After this she would have a cup of black tea with a slice of dry bread and then set off to the fields with a hoe in one hand and a can of water in the other. She never drank our water because she did not like the taste of well water. She always managed to find herself some special place where she would get clear water from the ground. She would dig a small hole in the ground and it would soon result in a little spring of water coming through. Sometimes the water looked milky in colour and that was when she liked it the most. It amazed me how she always knew where to dig to get water. It seemed like a little bit of magic to me. My grandmother seemed very happy and contented with her simple life and she never wished for more than she had. All she lived for was to work hard the whole day, come back home, take a bath and then see that there was food on the table for everyone. Her eating habits were a bit strange as she stuck to the things she had eaten as a child. She would eat the maize meal with us but would cook her own special stew on the side. She never gave this to us because she didn't want us to eat the food she grew up eating, which was all sorts of different insects and worms. The worms were called mapani worms, and there were flying ants, locusts, mice, beetles, and many other things you could never, ever imagine eating. Strangely though, when she cooked her special dishes we always wished for them and sometimes I would taste what she cooked, without her knowing. Sometimes she would end up sharing her stews with me because she was so afraid to see me cry. Of course, knowing this made it easy for me to get my way at times and I would play on her feelings and fears. After supper my grandmother would help us clean the dishes without saying much while we worked, and then she would go to bed on the floor next to the wood-burning stove. This would be the same routine for her each day except on Sunday, when she would make sure her dress for church was washed and so well pressed that it looked like she had put starch on it. She always ironed with an old-fashioned charcoal iron but she was so good at it that she never left the slightest trace of a black mark from the ash. As she prepared for church she would tie her hair back with a pristine piece of white cloth, and her shoes were polished till they shone brilliantly. Her slim black body shone too as she lavished herself with Vaseline, which she always used instead of lotion. After all these preparations she would set off to church, walking over ten miles. She would leave early to get there in the morning, then return back late in the evening. She would walk back into the home just in time to make a fire to prepare meals and boil water for the family to bathe. Every Sunday evening her routine of hard work caring for the family and working in the fields would start all over again, but she never once was heard to complain.

Although my grandmother worked so hard in the home with no modern appliances and so on to help her look after the family, she worked even harder on the farm. She always planted her own fields of crops and didn't allow anyone to help her weed them or anything. She did all this work on her own and even when the crops were ready to be harvested, she would put all the produce that was ready into big cotton sacks and carry them to the shed. This was a tiny hut that she had built herself out of wood, mud and grass. She would carry the sacks or buckets on her head. Sometimes these weighed over fifty pounds each but she skilfully managed this feat without spilling anything or losing her balance. She would take stock of everything she had, memorising it and keeping the details in her head. She was a unique woman and a good example for her family who all loved her so much.

My grandfather's brother, Uncle Charley, was a very quiet man who had lots of respect for people but he never liked talking to anybody—not even his own brother. He was extremely reserved. He loved to go hunting for wild animals every day with some of the farm workers. They would go out in the evenings mostly, with big torchlights. Uncle Charley was an avid gun collector, and loved to spend hours sitting and cleaning them. He was a man that had no time for women so he never got married or had any children. Marriage wouldn't have suited his personality as he was someone who loved to live quietly with no disturbances and seemed to prefer animals to people. He spent a lot of time taming some of the wild animals that he caught and making them into pets. His dog was always at his side and he treated it very well. Uncle Charley always dressed in an overall with big black army boots—I can't recall seeing him dress any other way. His beard and hair were always kept long.

My parents wedding day

I lived surrounded by my grandparents' five remaining children; the older ones had already left home. In total, my grandparents had nine children with two that passed away. My uncles and aunties were all a lot older than me and would always be too busy working, either in the fields or doing part-time jobs working for the white people in the area, to waste time with me. They were continually trying to make money, to save up and find a way to go to the capital city, Salisbury. I don't think any of them were really interested in farming and only ever helped out just to make some money.

Me in my Grandfather's car

The house we lived in had five rooms—three bedrooms, a sitting room and a small kitchen. There was a stove that used firewood, and paraffin lanterns for light because we had no electricity. I used to think that our sitting room was the most beautiful place. This was because my grandfather had most of the things imported from his home country—Britain. My grandfather slept in one of the bedrooms and only on occasions would my grandmother be allowed inside. My grandmother slept on the floor next to the stove, with two blankets on a mat with a small pillow that she had made for herself from old clothes. The second bedroom was for the boys, and the third room was for the girls. These bedrooms were very large, with straw mattresses and a small dresser to pack our few clothes in. We didn't have much in the way of material possessions and we were used to hardships like sleeping on straw mattresses. We used very stiff, scratchy, grey blankets but none of us minded this. Even my grandmother liked everything this way; nobody could force her to do anything she didn't want to do because she was a very proud woman, always getting her own way. She brought us up to know that we had white blood because this was so important to her. She wanted us to live and behave the way the English did, while she followed the ways she had been taught by her own parents. She never wanted to change and adapt to our ways. We never knew whether she could speak any English and even if she knew the language she would never have shown us. All she spoke in front of us was her native language, which we all understood and spoke.

As my grandfather got older he became very friendly with everyone—even the people who didn't like him because of his wealth. He spent his days laughing and talking to all the people who came to see him and there was never a day when he would get annoyed or upset. The only problem was that he loved to eat. He became less active as he got older so he gained a lot of weight and was obese. Even though he got a warning from the doctor to watch his diet, it didn't bother him. His reaction to that was that you have only one life and when it was his time he would go peacefully. He was not a lazy man; he was always keeping himself busy. He would spend his days in any of his shops, walking around his farm and keeping an eye out for his wife in her fields. He would collect some vegetables and fresh milk and then deliver to customers in town. He didn't have to rely on the strangers who worked for him as he had help from some of his children.

Every Sunday my grandfather would attend church and I would be the only one who went with him. This is when I truly began to take Jesus into my heart and I felt that he was my Jesus and this conviction was to continue for the rest of my life. We didn't go to the same church as my grandmother—we went to the Catholic Church while my grandmother went to the Methodist Church. I remember that I used to feel so proud when I sat alongside my grandfather in the front seat of his little old Morris motor car, with my hair tied in two bouncy bunches with large bright ribbons hanging from my head. On Sundays I would always wear the beautiful dress that the tailors had sewn for me with the materials my grandfather had imported for me from his country. My grandfather was proud of me and would tell me that I had taken the best out of the whites and the best out of the blacks and that was what made me look even more special.

On the side of his dresser my grandfather kept a picture of my mother, saying she looked just like Queen Elizabeth in Britain. I used to love to hear his stories about Britain and the Queen. This made me wish that one day I would meet the Queen, but all I could do was just play out the event—a very grand occasion, I was sure—in my head over and over again. He also told me that he had named me after one of his sisters and this made me a very proud child. I just knew that one day Britain would be my home, following my dreams and finding my roots.

This is what my grandfather always told me and that he was going to take me back home to his family to make sure I had a good education and a better life. This was a dream that both my grandfather and I hung on to throughout my childhood and talked about frequently on our trips to church.

Although life was not always easy, we were very privileged; we were not suffering like most of the local people in the area who were black. The white people always seemed to have everything. In those days the whites had big, beautiful, comfortable homes and they always had more money than mixed race and black people. Anyone who wasn't white was usually put into special areas, with houses that looked like match boxes. These houses were so small and ugly looking with most of them having flat roofs and cement floors. Outside they had small yards with soil that was so poor that it reminded me of river sand so it was difficult to grow things such as vegetables. The only jobs these people could find were low paying, like working for the white people cleaning in and out of the houses. I saw these houses and the lives they were leading and realised, even as a toddler, that I was very fortunate.

Everyone in the family played their part in helping to look after whatever needed doing, especially looking after all the animals that were in the farmyard. Even we children never complained about this because hard work was part of life and it was all that we knew. There was no real resistance to work in the family, as there was very little else to keep us occupied. There was no television or anything to keep us entertained and we didn't go shopping or to the cinema so sometimes working was just a way to help to pass the time.

My grandfather had a source of entertainment, however—he had a radio and a gramophone. He would listen to his radio first thing in the morning and last thing at night, always making sure he had spare batteries. He hated being without his music and would panic without it. His old fashioned gramophone was only used for special occasions—birthdays, Christmas and, of course, every Sunday after church. On Sunday afternoons my grandfather would sit in his big chair with a big cup of tea listening to the 78s that he had brought from Britain when he came to Rhodesia. The only interruption to this was when he had to sharpen the needles the machine used—and this he seemed to have to do every week. The gramophone was worked by winding it with a handle and he was forever replacing or sharpening the little thick needles that it used in order for it to sound properly. Children were never allowed to go near it because this was valuable property and both the gramophone and the old records were very delicate. My grandmother was allowed to polish it and she did an excellent job of it. There was never a speck of dust on it and it always looked brand new.

My best memories of the life we lived on the farm involved the land. Huge mountains surrounded us and there were lots of trees and a nice big dam, which we used for fishing or playing in. The dam's actual purpose was for irrigating the lands and it had huge water pipes leading to the fields, with sprinklers that would run almost all day. These sprinklers in action were such a pretty sight to see for a little person like me—the droplets of water sparkling like diamonds in the sunlight. Sometimes I was very naughty; I would take off all my clothes and scamper between the rows of vegetables just to get sprinkled on. I would be laughing and screaming as if I had a lot of children playing with me even though I was alone in the fields. I really enjoyed my solitary games. After running through the sprinklers, my wet, very long, straight hair hung at the sides of my face and made me look like a little mermaid—but with legs instead of a tail. On other days I would head for the mountains, just to find wild fruit to eat and I would look for some wild flowers to take back to my grandmother. I really do think I was being looked after by angels because I used to disappear for hours so that the adults had no idea where I was and I would just wander the mountains and fields all alone and no harm ever came to me. It made me feel as free as a bird.

When I had just turned seven and it was the beginning of school, I began to realise the differences between people. People asked me a lot of questions about my parents and, because this was something that nobody ever talked about in our family, most of the time I had to keep my mouth shut. If I talked about my family it made my grandmother very angry, resulting in me getting a good hiding with a stick on my legs. Then she wouldn't talk to me for a few days. I hated this punishment, even though I didn't really understand what I had done wrong, so I learned to avoid answering such questions. Despite this problem, I enjoyed going to school for the first time and I enjoyed being the best dressed. Having my grandfather drive me to school every day was such a privilege. None of the other children were driven to school—they all had to walk. When I sat next to my grandfather on the way to school, I would sit up straight and look very proud. I used to think that one day my family would be very proud of me; nothing would ever spoil my dreams of going to Britain one day.

For the next few months all was well. We were happy until, one morning in winter, disaster struck when my grandfather didn't wake up. He had died in his sleep, of heart failure. I think—and hope—that since he was asleep he hadn't felt any pain as he died. The only pain that was felt was by his family. And that pain was almost unbearable. My grandmother was so hurt, but didn't want anybody to see her cry so she withdrew from the family at this time. Uncle Charley looked like a ghost, his face so pale. He just walked about with his hands in his pockets as if in deep thought. It was so sad to see him like this. He had been very close to his brother. My grandfather was buried on a very cold winter morning and I was allowed to attend, as my grandfather had been so fond of me. My grandmother didn't believe that I was really old enough to attend a funeral so I had to get on my little knees and beg her to let me and, with my aunties helping me to persuade her, she finally gave in.

There were so many people who attended his funeral that they filled most of the cemetery grounds and spilled out along the lanes leading to the little church. For as far as you could see there were all the people my grandfather had helped and employed. They all loved him, an old white man—and this was the African people. It was a bitterly cold morning but I just thought this was the right kind of weather for his last time on earth because I sometimes used to think that he missed the cold weather that he remembered from where he grew up in England. When they were lowering the casket into the ground I fell to my knees and cried 'Please Grandpa, can I come too?' There was no answer to be heard, only my auntie pulling me away from the grave, telling me not to be silly. With my knees bleeding I was taken away and put in some corner until it was all over.

After a few weeks the whole family returned to the cemetery and planted some nice flowers on my grandfather's grave. There was never a headstone to show who was buried there; all we had to remember him by was a number. In my mind I believed he was still going to come back to me one day to say goodbye and I will wait for the rest of my life.

Life was very different for us all after my grandfather died. My Uncle Charley was devastated and really didn't know what to do with himself. He moped around and just couldn't seem to get on with his life in any way. After a few weeks he realised he just couldn't remain on the farm so he left to return to Britain. He felt he had nothing left for him and was desperately lonely without his brother.

I suffered a great deal during all this but in those days nobody noticed when a child was sad; my granny used to say a child should never be seen or heard when there were grown up people around. They were not supposed to speak about certain things. Whenever my grandmother had any visitors we were not allowed to come out of our rooms or make a sound till the people had left.

My questions and feelings wouldn't go away because there was no one to help me cope with them. I suffered in silence just like Uncle Charley, crying myself to sleep quietly without anybody noticing me, with the feeling that my world had also ended. I was lonely and afraid because I felt the only person in the world who loved me and understood me had died. I was uncertain about my future—who was going to look after me and spoil me like he did? The only person who had ever listened to me when I spoke had left me all alone with my grandmother and I certainly could not speak of any of my feelings to her. If I ever tried to broach the subject of my grief, I would get a terrible hiding. My life had changed.

I used to get some comfort at this terrible time by recalling the things my grandfather had taught me. I remember my grandfather telling me that in everybody's life there is a time to be born, a time to die, a time to cry, a time to laugh and a time for everything and that all I must look forward to is the promise of tomorrow. When I thought about all this I felt a little better knowing that this was his time and I knew that he would never like to see his little princess so sad. So I tried very hard to make peace with my little heart and stopped crying for a while. Looking back, I truly believe this was the beginning of the countless tears I have shed during my life, which I would always relate back to this time and to my grandfather. This was the first really painful experience in my life and I have remembered it all my life. Each time I shed a tear all these memories return.

2

A change in circumstances

Some time later the Government sold my grandfather's shops and the house. All his cattle went to auction, all the moveable things were auctioned off, and then they gave my grandmother little more than one month to move out. This must have been so painful for my grandmother. To be uprooted from her home by force must have been horrendous for her. Once again this brought back such painful memories and tears of sadness to the family.

When they read my grandfather's will, my grandmother was left fifty pounds and there was ten pounds for each of his children, but the rest of his money was sent to Britain to his family there. My granny was so shocked at having her possessions taken away and sold. To have then been left such a little bit of money in my grandfather's will was an even bigger blow. For a mother who had nine children with this man who she loved, who had worked hard for all her youthful days, this was a dreadful snub. As usual with my grandmother, all the stress and pain could only be seen in her eyes because this was the type of woman she was; she never wanted to show anybody her true feelings. She kept her pain and hurt to herself and some of the pain she felt more in the night in the privacy of her own room, where she would probably cry herself to sleep quietly making sure nobody heard her. I knew this because there were many days when her eyes were swollen and puffy and this was when I realized that not just my world but also my grandmother's world was damaged beyond repair. She became a complete stranger to everybody. She hardly talked and never laughed with anybody so the sound of laughter with the feeling of satisfaction and happiness left us all. It died the day my grandfather left us; the house even felt like it had an echo, with a feeling of emptiness like there was something missing.

We eventually left the house with what few things we could carry but we still stayed in the little town of Selukwe near the old farm. We managed to rent a small, three-roomed house with ten acres of free land and a river nearby. All the local people were so sympathetic to my grandmother for her loss, meaning the passing away of my grandfather. Nobody knew what had happened with the farm; they just thought my grandmother wanted something smaller. The little house my grandmother got was not even suitable for human beings to live in—it looked more like a chicken run. When we arrived my grandmother had to take a stick to beat me because I was refusing to live in a chicken run where, to my way of thinking, the white people kept their chickens. It was an awful shock to me to be brought to this dreadful place.

Me on the doorstep of my granny's house

At this point there were just four people living in the house because my other aunties and uncles had all left for the capital, Salisbury. That was the only place where high paying jobs were fairly easy to find and also there was family to help with living expenses for the first few months while they got settled. None of the family ever sent money or groceries to the family left behind in Selukwe, yet they all knew how we were suffering. One of the few things people who have everything never realize is that the next person might need some help. I suppose life is so complicated for everyone that it is easy to forget the needs of others, but if there is no sincerity and thought for the family then I don't know what else there is. It seems so important to me and I was so surprised by the lack of thought displayed by my relatives when we were in this awful situation. I hope that one day I, and all my family, are going to be judged fairly.

Me (holding skirt), sister Wendy, brother Harold and a cousin

Our house had only three rooms—one bedroom where we all slept as there were no boys in the house, a sitting room and last of all the little kitchen where my granny still slept on the floor near the firewood stove. This was the only thing she had managed to take illegally out of the old farmhouse, which she and her husband had owned. The roof of our new home was made of zinc and had very large holes in it, so when it rained the water poured in. We would get wet through and had to run backwards and forwards emptying buckets of water. During the rainy season we would sleep on wet blankets at night. The zinc roof and the typical construction of the house caused us plenty of other problems. As the sun heated up the roof during the day it would expand and when it contracted it would make a very scary noise—like a thunderclap in the night—and I would lie awake worrying about what was going to happen to us. When the wind blew it felt like the house was being uprooted because all the poles that held the house together would shake violently, with some of the roofing lifting right into the air. The sitting room floor was plastered with fresh cows' dung. This would form a hard surface as if you had used layers of cement. This type of flooring would last two weeks or more and would help to keep us warm. Sometimes, in winter, it would be very cold in the house because it didn't have the usual thick plastering made out of mud. One thing my granny taught me to do to try to keep warm was to put a stone into the fire and leave it until it became very hot, and then take it out and wrap it in some old clothes and place it in my little bed. This would warm me up while I slept.

Our drinking water was from a very deep well in the yard. It was about six feet wide and had no guards around it for children. I sometimes wonder why we never had an accident here as it only had a small zinc cover that was easily moved when we went for water or whiled away the time throwing stones at the frogs that lived in the smelly, green water. We always drank this water without a second thought—and without boiling it.

Going to the toilet was another traumatic experience while we lived here. My grandmother had got someone to dig a hole in the ground and then she placed a wooden block over it for a seat and this was the toilet to be used by the whole family. Every time I went into this toilet, I hated it. I would find that I became full of maggoty worms whenever I used it. These worms would grow in the body and my grandmother would keep inspecting it—prodding and poking it until she thought it was ready for it to be squeezed. This would leave a very deep, large hole where it had been eating away at my flesh. This was the most painful and disgusting thing for any young child to experience. I learned that the bush was a much safer place to use the toilet, so that's what I usually did.

After all the repairs to the house were finished it began to feel a bit more like home but I remember still feeling embarrassed when people came to visit because, I suppose, what we had before and what we had now were two totally different things. I felt the humiliation very sharply and it was obvious that my granny was hurting from the shame but this was a feeling we all had to get over. It was inevitable that sometimes we would think that maybe if we were white none of this would ever have happened. If we'd been a white family, of course, the social welfare would have looked after us after my grandfather's death and my granny would still have had her farm. It was my first real experience of the disadvantages of not being white and it was all a bit bewildering for a little girl.

It was a year later when the priest came to see my grandmother; he had received some bad news from Britain. A letter had arrived saying that Uncle Charley had died, that he had suffered a heart attack. I still believe that Charley could not get over the heartache he felt about my grandfather's death. Before he died he asked one of his relatives to write to the priest to pass on the message to his other family in Africa, saying he will always love us very dearly and kept us all close to his heart. He said he would never forget the good times he had had on the farm. His time in Rhodesia with his brother and all the family had been so very special to him.

After a while, life settled down and I began to love this place. There was a river nearby that made me so happy. I loved going swimming and messing about looking for things at the water's edge. Being by the river would give me a beautiful feeling of peace and joy, something you would never be able to explain. The running water sounded to me as if it sang a heavenly tune that only I could hear, while on the riverbank my aunties would be making clay pots. This was so interesting for me to watch. They moulded the pots with their hands and then the pots were heated in the fire to set them and then they were very useful items for us. We also washed our clothes once a week at the river. We would beat the wet clothes on the huge rocks at the water's edge, then put them to dry on the green grass that was blowing in the wind, singing its own tune to me. This made me so happy. I knew the beautiful tune was a gift from my Jesus. Within a short time our clothes would be dry and our bodies would also be washed. I found being at the river and all the things we did there so exciting and at the same time I was at perfect peace with nature. It was like being in heaven. When we were hungry we ate the berries from the trees that hung over the river. They were big, sweet and juicy and made a wonderful lunch. On the way home through the fields there were lots of grasshoppers. We all knew exactly which ones to catch. There were some that had big, fat, yellow eggs in their stomachs and when you fried this it was so delicious. My mouth waters just thinking about it. Although we weren't usually allowed to eat insects, worms and so on, my granny made an exception for grasshoppers because she said that it was better than eating meat. So each person ate according to how much they caught and this would sometimes be the only thing for supper. Both my aunties had to look after me while they went about their chores by the river and were not allowed to leave me alone as I was too young. On the way home there were guava and mango trees growing wild all around us in the bush. In Selukwe, I don't know why, but the best of all vegetation in Africa grows even though it has the coldest winter of all. For our toilet throughout the day we used to go into the bush—I think that's why there were so many guava trees!

There was always plenty to see just outside the house. It was best in the mornings when, with the sun barely risen, you would see so many different kinds of birds, of all colours, flying in huge flocks. They would swoop down to the ground and then soar upward again into the dawn sky. They would sweep within inches of my grandmother, as they looked for fresh things to eat from the ground. Just seeing this filled me with such joy and even at my young age I knew instinctively that something as beautiful as this had to be made by my Jesus whom I so strongly believe in. My little heart would pound as I watched and, despite our problems, my spirits were raised and I felt as happy and as free as these beautiful birds.

Our bathing facilities at this new home were just as primitive as our toilet but didn't cause me any problems. My granny used to boil water in a big metal bucket on the fire outside in the back yard. We then had to stand in the little metal bathtub and you would just soap yourself all over, then pour water over yourself (or my granny would help me, of course) to rinse off the soap. This happened everyday because we had to go to school and granny was very particular about us keeping ourselves clean, even though we lived in such poor conditions. If we had no Vaseline in the winter days, we would use soap to rub on our bodies. This was, so my grandmother said, just to keep warm and to look smart. We would then brush our teeth with the bark of a special tree that grew near the house. For me the worst part of getting ready for school was that there was no proper comb and brush for my very long hair. My aunties hated combing it and they always made me cry by pulling so hard that it came out in bundles. They would shout at me to be quiet and stop crying, thinking that I should be able to stand the pain. Even now my head is very sensitive and I don't allow anybody to touch it apart from myself.

After all this bustle and bother to get ready for school, the journey was hard and it did not make it any easier for me to accept that I had had to change schools and now went to a cheaper, less pleasant school. I had to dress in a thin cotton dress even in winter and then walk over ten miles to school with no proper shoes, with no jersey to keep me warm and, when it rained, no raincoat. Sometimes there wasn't even a cup of hot black tea to start my day. Some mornings, as I dragged my feet to school, I would dream of a hot meal. The teachers were mostly kind, though. They became very worried when they saw how thin I had become so they gave me fresh milk with a sandwich each morning at break time. It was lucky for me that the teachers liked me. I remember there was an albino girl called Venus in my class and the teacher hated her so much, that on occasion she would take a hosepipe and beat the little girl till she bled. Sometimes, in the winter, she would take the hose and douse her with icy cold running water, saying she did not wash herself properly. Sometimes, I would think that all this humiliation and pain happened to her because she was an albino. All this was done in front of the rest of the class and most of the children would laugh but this always made me so sad that I also cried. I tried to be her friend when nobody was watching but I was afraid that I would be hated as well. Nevertheless, I would give her half of whatever there was to share. In those days children used to get a hiding with a teacher's cane or sometimes with a rubber stick made from an old tyre. The teacher never showed any mercy or kindness and would not stop hitting an errant pupil until he or she saw you crying, sometimes wetting your pants if you had any. I never had any pants and to this day I still do not wear any. There was to be no sympathy on offer at home either—most of the parents would be very happy that their child got a good hiding because next time, they believed, he or she would try harder and do better.

At home, things got worse. My grandmother soon ran out of money and she was so desperate that we had to apply for Social Welfare. Fortunately, we were accepted and the help was given on weekly basis—just a very little money and some groceries. This would help the whole family every Friday and this became our special day—especially if they gave us a piece of meat. My granny would cut the meagre meat ration, counting the pieces as she did so in case one went missing. We would all sit around the table smiling with each other at this point because we were filled with anticipation of a good meal at last. Our main diet was maize cooked into a hard pulp and served with sour milk (or you could say rotten milk) plus a few boiled green vegetables with no oil or anything to make them nicer to eat. On some occasions, when granny's money hadn't stretched to last the week, there was nothing at all to eat. I remember that when we used the toilet during these very hard times, the colour of your stool would be green instead of brown because of all the green in our diet. But when we had meat we felt like royalty!

We couldn't afford to buy clothes for ourselves at this time either and the welfare helped us out here too. To my dismay, the clothes we were given were always second hand, too big or too small—never anything you wanted or would have chosen for yourself. One day my grandmother beat me up with a stick, leaving big marks on my body. The reason for this beating was that when I had collected the clothes that the welfare people had given us, I handed them back saying 'these things are all too big, ugly and old. Do you have something new that might fit us?' This incident was immediately reported to my grandmother, resulting in me getting beaten without any explanation. She was simply afraid that the welfare would refuse to assist us in future and she was terrified of what would become of us without their help. I accepted that was a good enough point and accepted the beating. Many children would have hated the person who beat them up, but I truly loved my grandmother and respected the way she thought. She believed that everything should always be done in a positive way. Unfortunately, my outburst did cause a misunderstanding with the welfare people. The one lady who was usually very kind to us became cruel and hard and she only gave us just a little of everything we used to get. The quantities of food and clothing were reduced so much and caused us such hardship but there was nothing we could do. This made me feel so guilty towards the others, but also gave me the secret satisfaction of showing everyone that I didn't like wearing rags. My pride had cost us dearly. My guilt and fear for the family's future made me wonder what had happened to all the money that had been saved for me by my grandfather. Had this also been sent to England? Every night I cried silently in my bed. I didn't want my grandmother to catch me crying as this would have caused a lot of trouble in the house and I felt that I had already caused more than enough.

Life became hard once more and we all had to help out in the family. We all had to do our daily chores and mine was going to look for a bundle of dry wood for the fire and my grandmother would come home to check that it had been done. After this we were allowed to do whatever we wanted. Every day I would come straight home after school and be very lucky if there was anything to eat because we now only ate once a day—that was in the evening. If we had a cup of tea it was always black and to this day I prefer black tea with dry, unbuttered bread. This daily existence made me very tired and listless.

In spite of being so tired I still had the energy to go next door where some white people called Mr and Mrs Cluty, who were in their sixties, were staying and who really liked me. I worked cleaning the lawn and they paid me five pence plus some lemons—they owned an orchard of lemon trees. The money I earned was a lot of money for me at this time and I kept it hidden for sweets or half loaf of bread that the shopkeeper would cut in the centre and fill with lots of fresh cream. I can feel that now—it was so enjoyable, digging my teeth into that fresh bread with lots of cream covering my lips, sucking each and every finger. To wash that down when I got back home with the lemons I'd earned, there would be some fresh lemonade—but with no sugar, of course.

I enjoyed working for the Cluty's next door, who were now getting so fond of me that they were beginning to buy me things like clothing. These gifts had to stay hidden because I was afraid to show my grandmother. I pleaded with the family not to buy me anything but could give them no reason why and this made them very suspicious. I still continued to work every day after school, even managing to save up my pennies to buy a new jersey for school. One day they bought me a bull terrier puppy and a tennis ball as a present. I fell in love with the dog instantly and called him Tessie. Of course, I could not hide a dog from my granny so I told her about it and she was OK with it. She could see how much I loved it. It wasn't easy keeping a pet under those circumstances. I didn't have much to feed him on so his main diet was *sadza* mixed with salt or sour milk and even this wasn't available on a regular basis but he was very healthy and strong and never left my side.

When I left for school in the morning, I would have a big problem, as he would try to follow me to school. I had to chase him back, put him into the house and then run as fast as my legs would carry me so that he couldn't come after me. My granny would tell me that when she opened the door he would run around like a crazy thing trying to find me and then, when he realised I'd gone, he would start howling as if he was crying. He forgot about me after a while and got on with his happy little life on the farm until I came home from school in the afternoons. Then he would be so happy to see me—we'd have a great reunion every day, making such a fuss of each other. I did love my Tessie so much and would rush home after school to play with him with my new tennis ball. Sometimes he would come along the road to meet me as if he knew I was coming and I would share with him anything I had left to eat—even if it was only a few sweets. I would run home and get changed, then go out to play ball with him. He did this very well, giving me the ball back every time I had thrown it for him to catch or fetch. But one day disaster struck. He caught the ball perfectly but then, instead of putting it neatly back at my feet, Tessie started choking. He had got the ball stuck deep down in his throat. I started to shout and scream for help but by the time my granny arrived back from the fields, Tessie was dead. I cried and cried for my best friend. Who was going to play with me now? My granny and I buried the poor dog that same day at the back of the house. I don't remember when I stopped crying—it must have been many days afterwards. I thought that I didn't ever want anything to love and look after again as I just knew it would die too if I did. As I grew up and dealt with life's other problems, I forgot about Tessie but one night in September 2005, when I was thousands of miles away from my granny's farm where Tessie died, I dreamt about her. This was over forty years later and I still feel like crying. This is another of those memories that

I have stored away in the back of my mind. Maybe Tessie was just coming to me to say goodbye to an old friend.

The Cluty's later gave my grandmother some trouble. They reported her to the police, saying she had stolen me. They truly believed this because, they reasoned, a 'white' child should not be living with a black woman, so something suspicious must be going on. The approach of the white police towards my grandmother was awful. They bullied her with their questions and showed her no respect at all. When my grandmother refused to let me go, they took a stick and struck her across the face, leaving a long cut across her eyes. I think she should probably have had stitches in the wound but she just left it to heal on its own and it left an ugly mark. The police officers seemed to realise that their behaviour had gone too far and at this point they just asked for my parents' address, saying they would contact them. This trouble had all started because the Cluty's had met with my grandmother and explained to her that they loved me and wanted to give me things. My grandmother refused for me to be adopted by them and that's what started all the hatred. The end result, apart from my grandmother's face being scarred, was that I was not allowed to go to see them anymore. So, there was no more half bread or sweets or lemons and this made me cry because losing friends that treated you like family was painful.

It was also during this year that I fell ill with diphtheria and I was rushed to the nearest hospital. I was barely able to breathe so my parents were notified. Before this, I had doubted that they cared at all what happened to me so I was surprised when my father rushed to Selukwe that same day. When he arrived at the intensive care unit at the hospital, the doctor said there was no hope. My father wasn't ready to give up hope for his daughter though, so he suggested that 'since she can't breathe why not make a hole in her throat and put in something like a pipe for breathing'. Apparently, the doctor jumped up, agreeing with my father and saying that was a good idea. In this way my father probably saved my life, because it wasn't long after that my condition got better. The operation left an ugly scar on the lower front of my neck. When my father saw I was making progress, he returned straight away to Salisbury because he had to get back to his work.

I returned home to my granny from hospital, not happy but a sad little girl. I would stare into the sky, singing all the songs taught at home and school and remembering how good it was when grandpa was alive. I repeatedly asked myself why I was staying with my grandmother and not with my parents. They now had three other children whom I wanted to get to know. I would pray each night to Jesus to help me to see my family. I thought that my brothers and my sister were having everything nice for them, so why not me. All this made me feel very miserable and my life changed. My trips to the river became less, I was just sitting at home playing with my rag dolls and moping about the house crying. I went from a jolly little girl to someone looking so miserable and with none of the excitement for life that children should have. All I wished was that I could fly alongside the flocks of birds because they looked so happy, chirping to each other. My aunties could see this happening to me so they wrote a letter to my mother explaining the whole situation to her.

For the next few months I was getting more and more miserable and started to give my granny a lot of trouble. I refused to go to school or even to take a bath. My idea about the bath was that she should get me a bath like the one my sister and brothers were using at their home in Salisbury, as this was only fair in my eyes—I know now that I just didn't understand the problems my granny faced. I refused to suffer any longer and so, at the age of ten, I went on strike. Now I refused to eat food. I would go into the bushes looking for wild fruits and eat them quickly. Then I would go back home refusing the food my grandmother made for me. I would be very dramatic about it, making like I was about to die with starvation. I even stopped allowing anyone but me to comb through my long black hair.

After a few more days of crying, sitting on the floor playing with my rag dolls I looked up and got a shock, seeing my father, mother, brothers and sister coming down the road towards the ramshackle little house. This was such a happy moment in my life. I felt so shocked that it was as though I was glued to the ground. My mouth felt frozen, it just wouldn't open. After a while, a rush of embarrassment passed through me. Just imagine, they all looked so smart and clean while here I was, so dirty, dressed in raggedy clothes. My immediate thought was to wash in the river. I rushed into the house, collected my school uniform (which was my smartest dress at this time), and ran with some soap as fast as possible down to the river. I didn't know that my brothers and sister were at my back, following me. As I jumped into the water I finally realised I was not alone. After that, all you could hear was the sound of happy children enjoying themselves, splashing in the river and eating wild fruit from the trees above the water. This must have been about the best way to get to know my family. All I could think was that my Jesus had answered my prayers! I still hadn't stopped crying but this time my tears fell into the water and they were tears of joy.

That night we all sat around the fire, you could just imagine how wonderful everything had become—it felt like a real family reunion. The little house was packed with people and full of the wonderful smells coming from Granny's big black pot on the fire, cooking a wonderful meal of chicken stew (which we were only given on the most special occasions). One thing I can truly say is that an African lady really knows how to fry a chicken and the memory will stay with me forever. It's the tastiest dish I have ever eaten in my whole life. An African cook wastes nothing and everything on the chicken is eaten (even the intestines) and the feathers are saved for stuffing pillows. Before I went to bed, I sneaked away quietly to use the toilet at the side of the house. After I had finished I found a shovel, dug a hole in the backyard and buried all my little rag dolls that I had made myself and played with for so long. I also buried all the other little belongings that were worthless but which I treasured. I thought one day that I would return and dig them up again. I did this because I couldn't bear the thought of anyone looking on my treasured possessions with scorn, seeing these cherished things that I thought of so dearly as a load of rubbish. That night we all slept so peacefully—all bundled together like puppies. I certainly didn't forget to thank my Jesus for giving me back my family and that night I slept with a smile on my face for the first time in many months. I knew my family cared about me.

3

On the move

The days following the reunion with my family were just like a dream—a wonderful dream come true. My brothers, Harry and Kenny, and my sister, Wendy, just loved my granny's place. They wanted to spend the rest of their lives out here with granny, telling me that one day I would be sorry that I was leaving. But, of course, at this time all my thoughts were on getting to know my family and about having better things in my life. I was sick of the suffering we had all gone through and I especially wanted to say goodbye to social welfare and all the misery that had caused me.

My mother brought the wonderful news that I was to be a flower girl at my Auntie Erica's wedding. I would be able to choose my own dress and shoes and this was something so special that I felt like Cinderella even before I had started looking for my new outfit. All I needed now to make life perfect was a magic wand to make things happen faster.

I was looking forward to getting to know my family better and knew I had a lot to learn about my new life. I had seen very little of my parents in my young life but I loved them. My father, Graham, had been born at Stow Farm in the small town of Marandellas (now called Marondera in what is now Harare Province) to a white English father and a black African mother. His father had had eight 'wives' and my father was born to 'wife number 6'. He had attended boarding school and at 16 had got his first job in Salisbury—as an upholsterer and as a young man had played left wing for Arcadia United Football Club in Salisbury. He is a kind, generous man who always tries to help others and even now I always call him 'Daddy'. He had met my mother at his lodging house in Salisbury when she was visiting his landlady. My mother Jane was born at my grandfather's farm in Selukwe. She had long, straight black hair, had English features and appeared almost white. She was quiet, reserved and hard-working and she always cooked her own kind of food, which was mainly English style. I believe that she was the backbone of my father's success in farming and when she died he lost all his riches. She enjoyed a drink and loved listening to music—especially Charley Pride. My mother was very strict with her two daughters—Wendy and me—but her four sons were allowed a lot more freedom. When my parents came for me I was a very proud little girl. Being a family of mixed race, we suffered prejudice from both sides. In Rhodesia at that time everyone was put into categories—white, black or mixed race—and had to use facilities such as transport according to their colour. The white people were considered superior to us and the black people sometimes resented our white appearance.

After a few days, the day of our departure arrived and we woke up very early—before six—to have breakfast and pack my clothes. My mother was so embarrassed that there was nothing worthwhile that she could pack, and in the end I just wore my sister's dress and shoes. They fitted me even though she was one year younger. I could see the pain that my mother felt at my suffering from the look on her face as she looked at me dressed up in my sister's things. She certainly looked glad that she was taking me away. It made me unbelievably happy to see just how much they all loved me and this is what my prayers had been all about for the last weeks. I thought my dreams had been lost and, even worse, I thought I would not see my family again. I feared that they did not care enough to save me. But now, all my prayers had been answered at once.

Going away from Selukwe was so exciting. It was the first time I had been on a train; in fact, it was the first time I had been outside the little town. We all had to carry blankets to sleep on the train. This was when it suddenly struck me just what I was leaving behind, and sadness began to mix with my happiness. As I looked out through the window of the compartment, I felt an empty feeling and a deep pain went through me. I thought about all the things that I loved and would miss. The thought of never seeing our little plot, my beloved granny or my rag dolls again—all the lovely old familiar things—brought tears to my eyes. I knew now that I would miss my wonderful life—playing in the river, eating wild fruits, climbing the mountains looking for wood and, most of all, picking wild flowers for my granny—and these thoughts brought such a wonderful feeling of love and pride for her. I knew I would miss my grandmother's comfort when I was feeling lonely or sad, when I would crawl into her bed on the floor and cuddle up to feel her warmth. Sometimes I would sing till I fell asleep and I knew how much she loved my songs because not once did she ever say keep quiet. I was determined that I would always remember what my grandmother had taught me to believe in—telling the truth and doing things the correct way. I knew, as the train made its way to Salisbury, that nothing was ever going to change this. Even in this short period of time that I had been with them I could see already that things were so different between myself and my family. Lots of times I noticed that my parents did not discipline the children strictly and sometimes this made me feel angry. Being the new child in the family, I somehow knew that it was too soon to talk about these things. When I felt this way I would just have to visualize the flocks of birds that flew around my granny's little plot and this made me feel better.

We arrived in Salisbury the next morning with the conductor wakening us up saying 'arriving in five minutes' in a very loud, commanding voice, so we all rushed to get our things together and we jumped off the train. For me it was a whole new world. It was so strange to have noise all around me. It seemed all you could hear was fast-moving traffic, people shouting and, from the industrial side, all kinds of noises. I held tight to my mother's hand when we were crossing the road to look for a bus. I was afraid that I would be trampled on or run over by one of the hundreds of cars and buses that went whizzing by us. The traffic made me feel dizzy and I started to wish that I had never come. This new world wasn't just strange; it was frightening.

We eventually arrived at my new home and I immediately liked it. It looked so big and beautiful to me, with three bedrooms, a kitchen and a bathroom with the biggest bath I'd ever seen. Best of all, the house had electricity so we had a nice, clean electric stove with a kettle for making tea. We had proper beds with nice mattresses with huge soft pillows (nothing like the ones I had become used to at my granny's that were stuffed with straw and old clothes). I was thrilled to see a little radio as soon as I entered the house and my mother turned it on straightaway. As soon as I heard the wonderful music, I began to dance around the room, demanding that everyone look at me—I felt like a princess at long last.

That night I bathed for the first time in my life in a real bath with hot and cold running water. I will never forget how special it was. I splashed water all over the floor as I enjoyed my bath and pretended to swim in the lovely warm water. We had a nice supper of beef stew and rice cooked by my mother. This was the first time I had eaten rice—I believed that only rich people ate rice so I knew that I was rich at last. I was so happy and contented that night when I went to bed and sank into a proper pillow. I'm ashamed to say I forgot to thank my Jesus and fell into a deep sleep as soon as my head touched the pillow.

In the morning everybody else was still fast asleep but I was awake before daybreak. I always woke like clockwork first thing, before daylight, to say my prayers and comb my very long hair. Looking into the white ceiling above me to pray, I suddenly missed my old ceiling full of holes with just a peep of daylight showing through. I got up and crept to the window. Looking through, there was nothing to see apart from houses—not even a single tree or birds. This was my first taste of homesickness but I knew I had so many other things to be grateful for and I was so happy.

My sister and brothers had to be forced to get up as they were so lazy. I found this very hard to believe and was amazed that they cried about everything they had to do. None of them ever said prayers and eventually they teased me and called me names like 'holy smoke', 'square in the box' and 'old woman', but this didn't worry me as I loved them too much to get angry.

As soon as everyone was up and dressed, my mother told me to change into one of my sisters' dresses to go out shopping with her to buy a few things for me. I quickly put on the dress and shoes and combed my hair and announced I was ready to go shopping. My sister started laughing at me because I had not put on any panties. I didn't think this was really necessary because this was something we never did back home. My mother came to my aid and told them not to make a fuss and we went shopping together, getting dresses and all sorts of things for school.

My father had a very good job as a welder and was paid a good salary so he eventually bought a car. We would go for days out every so often, seeing different places. It was so interesting for me as we passed through the different neighbourhoods and villages. I learned the way people behaved—it was a really different culture to the way my grandmother brought us up. I was determined to learn everything as quickly as I could because school was about to open.

My parents enrolled me into a new primary school, which I enjoyed because by this time I was a fairly clever student. It was a thrill for me having everything new—not second hand—and it also gave me some confidence and pride. The only problem I did have at school at this point was in trying to cover the scar from my diphtheria operation. I thought everyone would be looking at my ugly scar and it made me feel embarrassed, so I would put an elastic band around the inside of my blouse collar so it would pull the collar tight to my neck. This did the trick in covering the scar but it would often leave me feeling breathless and faint. This was only a small problem though and I enjoyed going to school. Having this chance to get an education was so important to me. It seemed that all my dreams were falling into place at long last. I also dreamt of going to Britain to see where my grandfather lived, see where Uncle Charley was buried and of being a famous person one day.

It was at this tender age that I thought about ways in which to make some money. I used to take my mother's sewing machine and use it to patch together little pieces of cloth. This cloth I collected in great big bags thrown away at the material factory next door, so my materials cost me nothing. My sister and everyone laughed at me but I persevered. I sewed beautifully coloured bedspreads, like blankets, which I sold to the black ladies who came around selling vegetables. They were glad to buy my lovely bedspreads because they were too poor to buy blankets in the shops. At this time I was not even eleven, yet I would often have a long line of customers at the door. Everyday my sister and brothers and I had sweets bought with the money I earned. Sometimes, if my customer had no money, then we would exchange a bedspread for some green vegetables and this really helped my mother who now never ran out of vegetables.

About this time, I began to realise that my parents had a problem and the problem was growing. They loved to buy beers and drink. Eventually, they would go out to the pubs, leaving me with the younger children to look after and with the cooking to do as well. On some occasions they would take us all in the car to their favourite pub, leaving us to wait in the car for hours, looking at all the nonsense on the streets. When we moaned that we needed to go to the toilet, my father thought of a plan. He made a hole in the floor of the car—just leading to the ground below—and this was our new toilet. When we were hungry they would buy us some drinks from the pub and give us a loaf of bread to eat—this would be our supper. Being the eldest, I would try to make the others behave while we were waiting. On the odd occasion that I would try to correct my two brothers they would hide in the bushes by the side of the road and throw rocks at me. I would run home and go straight to my room and say nothing. My problem was that, although my sister and brothers liked what was happening, I didn't. I hated it because my grandfather and my grandmother had taught me differently, so I knew that what my parents were doing was very wrong. But there was nothing I could do. I'd been brought up to know the difference between right and wrong but my upbringing had not allowed me to voice my true feelings about things. I didn't know how to say anything about the situation at home either to my parents or to anyone outside the family. Maybe if I had things would have been different.

With what I saw happening to my family, I started going to church every Sunday and on Fridays going to confession. The priest, called Father Thomas, got to know me well. This priest was responsible for all the mixed race children in that community. Later on I made my first holy communion and asked Father Thomas if I could become a nun in the Roman Catholic Church.

He agreed so I started my lessons and he took some photographs to send to Rome. The plan was that when my initial training was over my next lessons would be in Rome. Father Thomas said that he would make sure of this. I was so committed to this idea that I worked harder than ever. I put a lot of effort into my lessons in the church and kept up with my schoolwork too. I carried on with my bedspread business, never forgetting to pick up my pieces from the factory and then doing the sewing in the evenings so as not to disappoint my customers. I spent so much time working and studying that I never had time to play like other children.

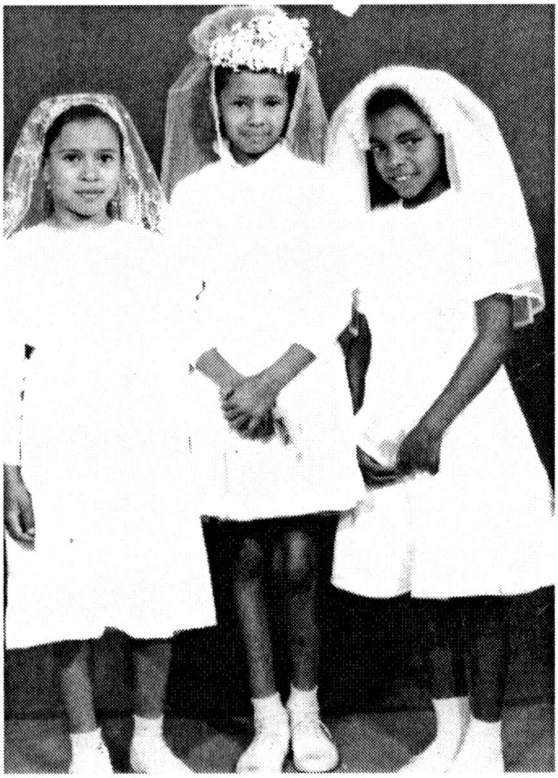

Me (on the left) with two friends making my first Holy Communion

The more money my father earned at work the more my parents drank. We started to move house frequently because of the problems their drinking caused so we lived in lots of different areas. Our schooling was badly affected because we always had to change school. I went to four different primary schools, but this never stopped me from going to the same Sunday mass with Father Thomas. During my last year in primary school, my father and mother started fighting nearly all the time. I tried to protect my mother by shouting at my father but this resulted in me getting beaten up as well and I would often wet myself during these episodes. Sometimes I would be unable to go to school at all because my body would be covered in blue marks and I was in a lot of pain.

This was a nightmare time for me and all the more difficult for me to bear because I had thought that life was just perfect when I had at last been able to come and live with my family, but while all this was happening my sister and brothers would just hide under their blankets very quietly. This was their way of coping with the situation. When all was quiet, it was time to get rid of the evidence of what had gone on there. I was left with my aching, wet body to try to get clean and my mother would be covered in blood, sometimes swollen from head to toe and there would be pools of blood all over the floor. I would get on my hands and knees and scrub until I left no trace of blood to remind us of the incident. Always the blood would be diluted with my tears, while my mother would just lay on the side with not even a stitch of clothing on but covered in blood. I will never know why my father always took her clothes off when hitting his wife. It just made everything much harder to bear for me and, of course, for my mother. For days after each bout of violence, I would have to be the cleaner and the cook and also look after the younger children. My mother was frozen in her fear and disbelief. She was so afraid to see a doctor or report what had happened to the police. She did not even tell her own sisters and brothers what was going on.

At one point, this situation became so bad that my mother moved out and went to stay with one of her sisters. She told my father that the drinking had to stop or she would divorce him. But he did not stop—he carried on even worse than before, because this time he had girlfriends as well. On one occasion he went out with his cousin and two girls. His cousin was driving but apparently they were all so drunk that he just couldn't control the car and they had an accident. One of the girls died. She was my father's girlfriend. He was in shock after the accident and could not remember how his cousin's false teeth came to be in his pocket when he arrived home with his clothes all messed up. The teeth looked so scary. They were full of blood, with something like meat stuck in them. My father then asked me to wash the shirt he had been wearing. This terrified me completely and sent me straight into a panic. I started running—without my shoes—on a gravel road to where my mother was living with her sister. This was over ten miles but I ran non-stop, so when I finally reached my auntie's home I fell to the floor crying. I begged my mother to return home to look after the children. I was so frightened that my schoolwork was suffering and I felt I couldn't cope with doing the housework as well. I also threatened my mother by saying that if she would not return I was no longer her daughter. My mother finally bowed to this pressure and returned with me to talk to my father. They came up with proper arrangements to save their marriage for their children's sake. After the talk with my mother, my father looked around at his children and I saw tears in my father's eyes for the first time. It made me realise that somewhere deep down in my father's heart he did love my mother and that he was sorry for all the things he had done in the past. The regret and love that we could see in our father's eyes helped to heal the hurt he had caused us all.

After this we once again moved to a new area, into a very large house with lots and lots of rooms. My mother ran this place as a small boarding house and she had lodgers, some of whom were soldiers. Some of them drank a lot, but they always paid their rent and my mother and father saved this money.

After this difficult period things started to go much better for us as a family. My father had another promotion at work and became the Foreman with a big wage increase. He seemed to take his responsibilities seriously and cut down on his drinking in the pubs, just drinking at home. This made life better for all of us. It wasn't long before the firm he worked for offered him a loan to buy a house. Instead he bought a farm called Travellers' Rest, which was about 30 miles from Gwelo (now known as Gweru). It had over a thousand acres, a beautiful orchard and, not far away, a river. Just hearing the sound of this lovely little river made me itch to go off and explore. The house had three bedrooms with no internal doors. Some of the windows had no glass in them and were boarded up and the zinc roof was full of holes but despite all these faults, I thought it was the most beautiful property my father had ever bought for his family. It reminded me of my granny's place in Selukwe about 40 miles away. I can remember that at the entrance to the farm stood two huge gum trees and a broken farm cart.

The bedrooms at Travellers' Rest were so small that you could not fit two beds in them, so my sister Wendy and I had to share a bed. The entrance to the bedroom was just a small open space and my mother had to put a cloth cover over it, so visitors to the house could not see into the room. In the morning the whole room would fill up with light from the holes in the roof and through the big open space that was supposed to be a window. Outside the window my mother planted a big bush of a rose tree with the most beautiful pink roses that had such a wonderful smell. That tree always seemed to be in flower. Whenever I think of it now, I can imagine the branches dripping with the gorgeous pink blooms and I can almost smell the intoxicating scent. When morning came I just gazed at the little lights shining from above and enjoyed the smell of the roses and the sights and sounds of the little birds—mostly robins and bluetits—flying over to eat from the ground. It all just made me want to jump with joy and explore everything. There was never a dull moment in my life at that time and I was completely happy and free.

My Father on one of his farms

Each weekend my parents went to look after the farm at Gweru, leaving me in charge of the family and the lodgers. I was so young and naïve at this time and had no idea that sometimes men can do very dangerous things to little girls. One of the lodgers called me into his room one Sunday morning and asked me if I wanted some sweets. He told me to sit on his bed and I thought nothing of this but suddenly the man locked the door and rushed over to the bed. I just felt the fear of death go through my body. I sat absolutely rigid with fright, knowing in that instant what was going to happen next. I suddenly realised that this whole situation was very wrong. My tears just started falling in an uncontrollable stream onto the front of my dress. Suddenly I heard the faint sound of my father's car coming down the driveway. This filled me with joy and relief and I leapt from the bed. I managed to unlock the door and escaped my captor. Despite my fear and the certain knowledge that this man had been doing wrong, I crept back into the house, just like a thief, without telling my parents what had happened. This was yet another secret for me to keep.

It was soon decided that my mother would run the farm because my father was still working and also we children were in school. The distance between the farm and the lodging house was over four hundred miles. My father then had a little shop built at the Travellers' Rest where we sold groceries plus the local beer. The shop had two rooms and a front counter, with a side room for my mother to sleep in on her own. We children had the one room while the other room was used to store the shop stock. He also planted a lot of maize and vegetables so the farm needed a lot of workers. We were so happy on the farm that after a while of journeying to and fro we all cried to stay with my mother on the farm. We went to school with the local priest who used to take his children into town for school about twenty miles away. To keep us happy, my mother and father agreed to this and soon after we started our new school. We easily made new friends. This move meant that I had to repeat my last year at primary school but we all loved our farm so much that we made a lot of sacrifices.

Living on this farm with my brothers and sister brought a lot of joy into my life; we did all the things that any happy, normal children would do. Looking back, I can see that some of the things we did were dangerous. For example, we would take a large iron bath from the back yard. We struggled to lift it and to carry it down to the river. When the river was overflowing and running at a breakneck speed downhill, we would take turns to be put in the bath and launch it like a boat; then we would scream with fear as it carried us down the river. We could have been drowned in the rush of the water and some of the big rocks that were on the side could certainly have knocked us out. Nevertheless, this was our favourite game.

All went well here until one day my father left for Salisbury after a weekend with us on the farm. My mother was busy as usual, serving someone in the shop when suddenly some guerrillas burst into the shop and held her up at gunpoint. These guerrillas claimed that they wanted to overpower the white government and fight for their land, which the white man had stolen. They threatened to kill all those who did not listen to them and they demanded food and drink. My mother was terrified by talk like this and wondered how she could possibly get herself and her children out of it, but since she is a white she was forced to feed them, waiting till they had had enough of whatever they wanted. The abuse continued even as they ate their fill, calling her the child of a prostitute because her mother, being black, should not have married a white man. While all this was happening we children were underneath the beds hiding. I was so terrified that I wet the floor. Our workers were lined up in a row and the guerrillas screamed at them, demanding to know why they were working for someone who is not a black and which side were they on? These poor, defenceless people were beaten, one by one. One old man who worked for us was in so much shock that while they were beating him he shat in his pants. He was dripping wet and the mess he made caused the house to smell for days. Eventually, they left us but the guerrillas came back several times after this first time, knowing that my father was not there. They warned my mother that if she reported them they would kill all of us. Nobody said a word to the authorities about any of this. My mother should have left the very first time when this trouble started but she was a strong woman. She should have known that leaving was the only way to escape these ruthless people. The farm next door was set alight and the farmer and his wife killed. When my mother explained all this to my father, he made a quick decision to move us all back to Salisbury the following weekend. After my father left for Salisbury that day, the guerrillas returned that same evening, setting fire to one of the small houses where we kept the stocks of maize and vegetables. Everything was burnt to ashes. As our property burned, these men sat and drank their free beers as if nothing had happened. They usually stayed, drinking, until the early hours of the morning while we were hiding on the cold floor all the time, our eyes and ears wide open, expecting the worst each time, thinking we were going to be killed. We would not go to school for a few days after this trauma.

We moved back to Salisbury again, to the old school to finish my last year of primary education. I was then enrolled into high school and I found life there so exciting because I was allowed to make my own decisions. I felt very grown up sometimes. I felt I had lost that child-like innocence that I had had when we lived out in the country. Although we had moved to the capital, I felt a lack of security and freedom. I had the awful, gnawing fear that anything could happen at any time with the ongoing war with the guerrillas.

After all this, my father sold the Travellers' Rest farm for a good profit but, instead of banking the money or buying a house, he bought another farm called Caps Farm 1 (later on my father also bought Caps Farm 2—also known as Bendu Farm) from a Mrs Caps. The only thing I can remember about this lady was that she had a hundred cats, which we were left to dispose of. This new farm was again in Gwelo. I don't know why, but my father loved this quiet little town. He asked my granny to sell her small plot and stay on the farm with my mother to try and make a go of things. On the radio news all was very quiet so we obviously thought there would be no more problems with the guerrillas.

Caps Farm 1 consisted of a very large house, with eight rooms, and an underground bar where my father sold beer to neighbouring families. The whole place was really beautiful and had wall-to-wall carpeting, built-in cupboards and two enormous bathrooms with toilets. The outside had very large chicken runs, a place to grind maize to sell to the local people and there were lots of cattle, sheep, chickens and ducks. My father later built a dairy to add to the facilities of this substantial farm. Even with all this I did not feel at home, as I really missed the old farm. This new farm looked like a prison camp to me. It had an electric fence right around it so that if anybody were to try to break in they would be electrocuted. All went well in the beginning until, after a few weeks, the animals started vanishing or we found them dead in the field in the morning with the fence cut in places. We never found out how this was done; as the fence was electric it should have been impossible. In the days that followed we also found our dogs dead at the gate because they had been fed poisoned meat.

It was not long after this that my father was approached by some policemen, saying they were directed by someone who knew us. They said that my mother should come into the mortuary to identify some bodies. In shock, my mother and father jumped into the car and left. On arrival at the mortuary, my mother had to identify what seemed to my mother like two young children's badly burnt bodies. When she had a closer look she found that one of the bodies was her brother's only daughter who had been travelling with her boyfriend to the next town to see her mother. She had been going to proudly show off her new car that her father had bought her for her eighteenth birthday.

The bodies were subjected to a post-mortem and the doctor reported that my cousin's breasts had been cut off; she had been bayoneted eight times before being thrown into the car, together with her boyfriend, and then set alight. Apparently, this was all witnessed by a herdsman, who hid in some bushes while watching the horror unfold. He said that the guerrillas had enjoyed themselves, drinking beer while murdering these innocent young people. The police also found out that the guerrillas had jumped into the car and taken them by force while the young couple were filling the car with petrol. They then forced them to drive into the bush where they were so brutally murdered.

Later that night none of the people in the house could eat any food. We simply sat silently in shock or crying softly, unable to believe what had happened. As for me, I fell asleep crying for the only cousin whom I truly loved. This incident had such a dramatic effect on us all, but especially us children who learned about violent death for the first time.

My father was once again forced into giving up his farm and several other small farm properties. With what little money he had after all this, he bought a small plot in town that had a borehole with water and ten acres of land for irrigating. This time he was determined that he was not going to give these guerrillas any more chances to make his family suffer so he persuaded my grandmother to stay, taking the rest of his family back to Salisbury to start a new life once again.

4

Growing Up

On the 11th November 1965, fearing the British Government's desire to transfer political control of its colony from the white minority of just over a quarter of a million people to the black majority of nearly five and a half million, Prime Minister Ian Smith issued his 'Unilateral Declaration of Independence' from the United Kingdom. International condemnation and sanctions soon followed and this was the start of a prolonged battle by the guerrillas to gain power.

Me (front) and schoolfriends

So, here we all were in Salisbury at a difficult period in its history, starting all over again. The first few days at high school felt strange, but I felt very mature. I combed my hair differently and took up all the hems of my dresses like all the other girls. I was very concerned to follow all the fashions but I knew nothing could worry me because I really wanted to learn and I didn't care about what the other children got up to. In some peculiar way, I felt safe and cared for through my high school years because I just knew that my grandfather was watching over me and would take care of me throughout my life. I think I felt this way because he had never said goodbye, so I couldn't let go.

Our high school had three floors with lots of different classes teaching a variety of subjects. I enjoyed moving between these classes, climbing the stairs each time the bell rang, having eight different classes to go to. All of us students were given a locker where we kept our books. In mine I also kept all my papers and books from church. I knew that they would be safe there, out of the way of my brothers. If I had left them at home they would have torn up these precious things, making fun of me.

I did very well in most of my subjects, except English, which I was very poor at. However, all the teachers were good at helping students when they couldn't cope with the work and they would give extra lessons voluntarily after classes. At that time we had mostly white teachers and just a few mixed race ones. Of course, during this period of time each race had their own schools and my school was just for mixed race students. This may seem a peculiar concept now but for us back then it was normal and we just accepted that we didn't go to school with black children or with whites.

During the first year of school three very nice things happened to me. Firstly, I began to take part in sporting activities like the long jump, high jump, hurdles and relay and I always won. I just seemed to be naturally talented at all of these things although I spent a lot of my spare time practising. I would take home trophies and certificates and this success meant that I had lots of friends, including the teachers. My parents were very proud when I came home with my trophies and they displayed my things around the house, but they never once came to see me at the school sports day. This lack of support and interest was painful enough for me to bear but even more distressing was the fact that neither my father nor my mother ever encouraged me to carry on with my ambition. They never supported me in my desire to go as far as I could with this thing that I was so good at. The only things that they took an interest in were planting and drinking beer—nothing else.

Me and my sister Wendy on my Uncle Percy's car

The second lovely thing that happened when I was new at the high school was winning the annual competition where the children all voted on who had the best body and who was the prettiest girl in the school. Taking first prize in this made me very proud and I even thought that one day I might be the queen of Africa. I knew that my good looks came from my mother—she was certainly a woman to be admired.

The third good thing that happened to me during this time was meeting and falling in love with Ighsan—the headmaster's son. We met on the school sports field when they put the best runner from the boys with the best from the girls to run against each other. He won the race, of course, but he also won part of me that day. He won my heart and my mind. This was when I stopped going to church. I lost my interest in Jesus because I thought that there was no time for anything else in my life. I found that I couldn't stop myself thinking about this boy and I spent hours at the dressing table, combing my hair and daydreaming, until my mother had to chase me out of the room to do my chores. This innocent love and admiration from afar carried on for quite some time and I enjoyed the lovely, secret feeling it gave me.

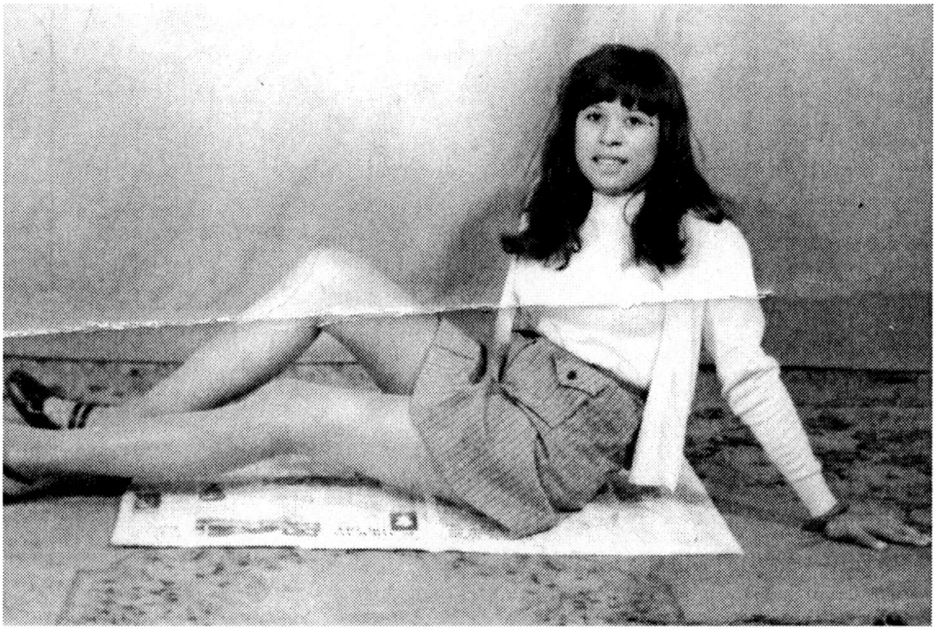

Me, aged 15

As well as being an exceptional athlete, Ighsan was very good at cricket and I used to enjoy watching him play. He was also a member of the army cadets but I didn't enjoy watching him take part in their meetings. He wore funny, large brown trousers that showed his long, skinny, hairy legs, with a large brown shirt and a huge, round, brown hat. The shoes that he had to wear made him look funnier still because they looked far too big for his feet. To me he looked just like a telegraph pole—so straight and thin that I felt sorry for him. At the time I didn't know why but I seemed unable to keep away and would always be trying to get a glimpse of him.

I think he felt the same way then because I would often see him watching me too. He had a special way of whistling so I always knew if he was around. He would pop into the classroom during my lessons, or would frequently pass my house—whistling so I always knew to go to the window to see this handsome Muslim boy passing by. He also came to many of the sporting events that I took part in. When I played netball I wore a very short dress and, as I had the most beautiful pair of legs in those days, many of the young men would come to watch us play and Ighsan would always be among them. Ighsan's sister Yasmine was the instructor and she would blow on her whistle and shout at me to stop doing ballet on the sports field—but she only did this when Ighsan was there. We would go on the school bus to play netball tournaments at other schools and invariably Ighsan would be on the bus, sitting next to his sister, just to see me play. We usually won these tournaments, as I was a very good player. Even my music lessons were disrupted. He would ruin my concentration on my violin playing by standing close by as I practised.

Things changed one rainy day while I was waiting for the rain to stop as I stood on the veranda of the school with my books in my hands. I had left my raincoat at home. As I stared out at the rain that looked as though it would never stop, suddenly someone put his arms around me from behind, pulling me towards him. He then gave me such a hard kiss. I had my mouth wide open in surprise and objection but I was totally enjoying it, knowing who it was. It was the headmaster's handsome son, Ighsan. I felt so shocked that I forgot it was raining and dashed out into the downpour. I ran all the way home with my schoolbooks in my hands. All I could think of was running home and jumping into bed. When I got home, I didn't even greet my mother but went straight to my room. I threw my ruined schoolbooks into a corner, got changed into my bedclothes and jumped straight into bed. I closed my eyes and vowed that, from this day on, I would never wash my lips again. I fell asleep dreaming of this handsome boy. The next day at school I was in so much trouble with the teachers but I didn't care. The feeling of this new excitement had made my heart lift and my body weak. I had to pay for new books because the ones I'd run into the torrential rain with were all spoiled and could not be used anymore. I was sent to the headmaster's office and he demanded to know what had happened. Of course, I failed to tell him that I had behaved so carelessly because his wonderful son had kissed me.

For the next year Ighsan still carried on trying his luck with me because he knew that I was different from the other girls. I was very difficult to win over. He wrote every day telling me how much he loved me; he engraved our names on most of the wooden desks of all the classes he attended; he wrote our names on the lockers of the pupils and on some of the very big trees that were in the school grounds. All this didn't go unnoticed. One day his father, the headmaster, called us both to the office. He asked us separately what was going on and we stuck to our story that we had no idea who was behind this. He asked if we were seeing each other but we denied this. He then gave us a lecture about relationships and explained to us that a Muslim boy should only go out with his own kind and that his wife would arrange in the proper tradition for his son to marry a Muslim girl. That night sleep didn't come easy to me and I lay in my little bed, crying. I kept thinking that Ighsan was only using me and this made me really angry. So, when he asked me to be his girlfriend despite what his father had said, I was taken aback. I needed to be sure of his feelings for me. I started thinking of things to test him and finally came up with three things for him to do to prove he really loved me. Needless to say, these were just the fantastic thoughts of a young girl upset and in love so I had no idea he was going to do all that I asked. Firstly, he was to jump from the second floor of the school building. This he did, breaking a finger in the process. Secondly, to jump in the dirtiest river in our area where they threw all the waste. This smelt like hell but, with his prefect's uniform on and holding his school case in one hand, he did this. He smelt like sewage all the way home. The third thing he had to do was to break a milk bottle and cut his arms. This is exactly what he did. After all this there was no going back on my word—I had no choice, so I became his girlfriend.

Now that I was his girlfriend we saw each other every day—both during school and after school. Things were made easier for us by the fact that the house he lived in was on the school premises, his father being the headmaster. We took advantage of this, always sneaking into his room. This is where it all began and where my innocence was lost. While we carried on our relationship, my parents had no idea what was happening. I was very careful to make sure that my parents didn't find out. I knew that it would cause a lot of trouble. My father kept a thick leather belt in his room and when he hit you with it you would see a multitude of different coloured stars. When it was my turn for punishment, I would collapse under the blows that he showered on me, always wetting myself and this was just for minor misdemeanours such as being late or speaking out of turn. He only used the belt when he was very drunk and didn't seem to know when to stop. So I could only imagine the type of punishment he would dish out if he found out about my relationship with Ighsan. I would perhaps expect to be killed so I was terrified of someone at home finding out about us.

Despite our fears of being found out, Ighsan and I spent all our spare time together. We couldn't seem to keep away from each other. One of our favourite places was a very big dam that we called Muckembuzi. It was over ten miles from the school and we used to cycle there together on our second-hand bicycles. This was our own private beauty spot—except that it was not beautiful. It was very dirty because it was where people used to throw away their rubbish and in some places it smelled awful but we were so wrapped up in each other that we didn't notice any of that at the time. We would find a quiet spot and lay our jackets on the ground and start kissing endlessly, enjoying the peace surrounding us with nobody watching us. Nothing else mattered. Time flew while we were at the dam and we were often surprised when it started to get dark. My parents did not allow me out at night so we had to jump on our bicycles and cycle furiously to get home. I would make my excuses to my mother before my father realised I wasn't there. I was afraid of my father and the big, brown belt he used to keep discipline in the house. This belt was a treasured possession of his as it had belonged to his father and had been used on him when he was a boy. It was kept in a safe place—he could always find it when he needed it and it was only ever used for this one purpose.

We had other ways of defying the curfew imposed by my parents. I would pretend to go to bed early, then lock the bedroom door. Ighsan would come to my bedroom window and we would kiss through the burglar bars till late in the evening. The next day I would struggle to go to school as I had had so little sleep. Many times I didn't attend lessons at school, as I would sneak away to be with Ighsan. We would find some deserted corner and kiss and kiss until my lips were sore. We didn't always get away with this, for, if we were spotted, we would invariably be reported to the headmaster—Ighsan's father. Not only was his father the headmaster, but my class teacher was Ighsan's sister and my Science teacher was his brother.

Once in a while, Ighsan's parents would give him some pocket money and we would go to the cinema. He always used to buy me a box of 'Maltesers' chocolates and a drink and I would feel so special as we never had chocolates at home so I would show off to my sister when I got back. Of course, we didn't watch many films. We would sit in the back row and start kissing as soon as the lights went down. We would spend the whole afternoon in the cinema, our limbs entangled and sometimes I would gasp for air. I felt as if this strange feeling of love would suffocate me.

On very special occasions Ighsan would give me a pretty chain or bracelet and this made me feel very proud. It was only later that I found out that all the jewellery that he gave me had been taken from his family's possessions. Of course, I had to hide the gifts in case there was any trouble.

We became known around the school as 'Romeo and Juliet'. Newcomers would ask about us as though we were filmstars and even the teachers grew to respect us after they had been unable to separate us as they could see the incredibly strong bond between us. Our reputation at school was enhanced, as we were not only a couple but also well known for our success at sports. We always brought home prizes and broke records when we took part in athletics meetings or played any of the other sports that we were keen on.

I didn't totally lose my senses during these early stages of my romance with Ighsan. Not only was I managing to keep it secret from my parents, I was also mindful that I needed to do well at school. I was in my fourth year, doing well and was about to sit my exams. (At that time it was called C.O.P.—similar to G.C.S.E.) As the exams got nearer I thought seriously about life and knew that having a proper education was more important than anything else. With the subjects I had chosen and the amount of time I needed to dedicate to my studies, I realised that I would have to give my relationship a break and concentrate on my schooling. I came to realise that we were doing too many of the wrong things and I began to study seriously.

The big day had finally come and I entered the examination room full of apprehension and feeling sick. But I had been preparing for these tests for a long time and I knew how important it was to give a good account of myself. On two or three occasions, while I was taking the tests, writing furiously, I had to excuse myself because of the feeling of nausea, but I managed to complete them. This was more than simply exam nerves. At this point I had my suspicions of what my problem was but I was much too afraid to tell my parents that anything was wrong so I borrowed money from a friend to see a doctor. He confirmed that I was indeed pregnant. This was my biggest nightmare. That night I cried myself to sleep; I knew that all my dreams had gone down the drain. Oh, if only I had listened to my parents and kept away from boys. My father was surely now going to kill me! I told Ighsan the next day and his reaction was predictable. He was shocked and full of fear about what his parents' reaction would be. They had high expectations for his future as he was a clever boy and the last born in the family.

For months I had been saving the small amount of pocket money given each week so that I could go and spend the school holidays at Auntie Margaret's place in Bulawayo. Now the school holidays were here and I was able to escape my parents' scrutiny and I went to stay with my auntie.

Staying with Auntie Margaret was so much fun and I began to relax a little. But the time came to leave and Auntie gave me some money plus a bus ticket to go home. She packed me a nice lunch for the journey and took me to the station in her little car. At the station I refused to get out of the car and started crying, refusing to go home. I told her nothing about my problem but we returned to her house. She didn't say a word, just went straight to the phone and spoke to my parents. She told them that I had refused to come home on the bus and that she thought it was because there was something wrong with me. I was probably pregnant. She had guessed my terrible secret.

Four hours later, I saw my father's big, ugly, green Vauxhall motorcar pulling up in the driveway. Just then I thought it was the ugliest car I had ever seen. I sat there inside my auntie's house and felt so embarrassed now that my parents were here to collect me. They sat down in Auntie's tidy little living room and called me into the room. Even before they had asked me anything, the tears rolled down my face uncontrollably. This confirmed their suspicions. My mother simply asked 'Is it true?' and I answered 'Yes', keeping my eyes down in shame. All that could be heard in response was the ear-piercing crying of my mother, like she was dying. This made me cry even more. My father was just as upset, but more controlled and angry too. He said that he could not believe that someone with so much determination could be so stupid, spoiling everything they had planned for such a long time. He just sat there shaking his head in silence for many minutes and looking so disappointed. Eventually, he looked up at me again and said, 'And now you have spoiled everything for yourself and you will never see Britain.'

His disappointment cut into me like a knife. It hurt me so much more than the beating I had been expecting. As I sat there, in tears, I even thought that he should have killed me, as I had feared he would. I felt I deserved it. Also, my dream of visiting Britain had turned to dust. We drove home in silence.

The very next day my parents went out in the car in search of my boyfriend. They didn't have to go far; they found him at the garage where they were filling up with petrol and he was having a soft drink. All they did was call him to the car, ordering him to jump in and then they drove the whole way to his house without talking. My father knocked on the door and when it was answered, he asked if they could come in and talk. Ighsan's father said, 'We have been expecting all this for a long time. We tried our best to stop them but failed; now they have to get married to save all concerned the embarrassment.' Nobody asked either of us if this was what we wanted; they just carried on talking about our marriage. They decided that there should be two marriages—one in the Catholic church and the other in the Muslim way—and that this should all be done as soon as possible before my pregnancy started showing. (The Muslim ceremony never took place as I refused to do it.) Ighsan's parents took over the whole situation. My father seemed bewildered but happy because he had had no idea that he was going to approve this marriage. I think he was a little intimidated with Ighsan's father being a headmaster. He obviously felt out of place and I think that when you are not with your own kind of people you are forced to agree with certain situations. So it was all agreed—we were to be married without delay.

5

Starting married life

As soon as everyone had agreed that we must get married, our families swung into action, planning a wedding that would do them proud. My mother bought me the most beautiful wedding dress I had ever seen and a veil with layer after layer of fine fabric, that was to be held in place by a delicate silver crown. There were pretty beaded shoes to match. It was decided that I would have two flower girls and two bridesmaids with a little pageboy and Ighsan was to choose his own best men. All the tailoring was to be paid for by my in-laws plus the band and all the food at the reception afterwards. Their generosity didn't stop there. Just before the wedding, some very smart furniture arrived for me from my future in-laws—a nice double bed, a dresser and a large wardrobe. These things were considered necessities for us to start married life, but as I stared in wonder at these luxurious items my thoughts were inevitably focused on who was going to sleep in the huge bed and with whom. I had never owned such things so I was really grateful to my in-laws, but I'd never had a new husband either so maybe my secret thoughts were understandable.

The wedding planning and organising went on around me and it seemed to go on forever, but the big day finally arrived. My hair and face were done to perfection and then I stepped into my beautiful dress. My waist had already expanded with my pregnancy so the dress was too small and they had to put me in a corset so that it would fit. When I was finally ready I looked like a little princess—something out of a storybook. My grandmother's face lit up with admiration and pride. I could feel the approval of my grandfather even though he was not there and I knew he would have been proud of me despite my mistake and my shame.

When I arrived at the Catholic Cathedral and saw all the people seated, waiting for me to arrive, I was terrified. I started to cry, wondering how they could possibly let such a child like me get married—I had always thought marriage was for adults only. As I entered the church on my father's arm, we passed a reporter who took some pictures of us. I later found out that one of his pictures was chosen by a newspaper agent as 'Bride of the Week' and this was to be published in the following week's newspaper. One thing that made me feel a little better was that it was Father Thomas who was conducting the marriage ceremony—the same priest who had baptized me and in whose church I had made my first holy communion, and then did some training to become a nun. I found his familiarity comforting when I was struggling to cope with the elaborate ceremony that I had found myself in the middle of and when all around me were people I hardly knew.

Our wedding day

After the church ceremony was over and Ighsan and I had been declared man and wife, we all went to the reception that was held at the Arcadia Community Centre, near our house. It was such a big reception that even the Mayor and his wife attended, my new in-laws, the Jenkins', being very important people. It all went surprisingly well. There were two bands and the guests danced and ate and you could see that everyone was enjoying themselves. At about ten in the evening my parents came to collect me and my new husband, saying it was time for us to go home because I was pregnant. I resented this as I just thought they were treating us like children, but at the same time I was happy to be going home to try out our new double bed and also to have some peace and quiet. It had been decided that we should live with my family until we could afford a place of our own. I hoped that, at last, I would get the chance to talk to my husband about all that had happened. This would be the first time in a long time that we would really be alone to share our feelings.

So in love!

Now, with the excitement of the wedding over, married life could begin and we had so much to learn. Everything seemed so strange. That first night I found sleeping very uncomfortable. I had grown up with my granny in an atmosphere where I was made to feel guilty if I enjoyed myself. As usual, I kept all my feelings to myself. Sleeping together in our lovely double bed was a brand new experience. We were so shy of one another that even sleeping together just sent a cold shiver down my spine. Getting any sleep at all was so difficult because we would be so stiff, we just couldn't relax. I also spent many hours awake in our bed wondering what was going to happen next in my life and worrying whether a forced marriage could possibly work out. At this time I discovered that my new husband wore two of almost everything—two shirts, two pairs of trousers. He did this to try to appear bigger than he actually was. I think that he would have worn two pairs of shoes too if he could. Maybe this is one of the reasons why I felt so shy and embarrassed when he was getting undressed—I would always pretend to be doing something else. Even very simple things, that most people take for granted, caused me problems. Being sixteen, I had never known any other boy. I had come into the marriage completely without experience. My new husband was barely seventeen years of age so he couldn't always help me with my worries and insecurities. For example, I didn't know how to kiss. My aunties had told me that when you were kissing a boy, you should put all your saliva into his mouth all the time. Of course, they meant this as a joke but I had no idea so this is how I used to kiss Ighsan. When we kissed I would have to continually rush out of the room for a glass of water.

By the time I was seven months pregnant we were just beginning to get used to married life. I loved becoming so close to my husband and we felt so happy with each other. As newly-weds, we would lock ourselves in our room for hours on end and become oblivious to the outside world. We would even forget to eat sometimes. We just sat holding each other as though we were afraid to separate even for a second. Our love had blossomed into something so great. Ighsan used to kiss me with so much pressure and passion that he would tear my lips.

We had great fun going shopping all the time for baby clothes, knitting baby sets and packing them away. Nearer the birth, I realised that we had collected over forty jerseys—jerseys of all different colours—and not much of any other sort of clothing. We decided that the baby was to be named Shane after the character in the 1953 western film 'Shane' starring Alan Ladd that I really liked. Late one night I felt a sharp pain in my stomach and when I got out of bed, water ran down my legs. I suddenly realised that the baby was on its way. I was only seven months pregnant so this caused great panic. We just had no idea what to do, so we needed help—and fast. By the time we woke up my father, I was bleeding heavily and I was taken by car, screaming with pain, to the hospital.

After a very short time at the hospital I gave birth to a baby boy. No one had ever mentioned to me about the afterbirth, so when I was pushing and the afterbirth also came out, I was shocked and frightened. I was screaming, thinking I had pushed too hard. I thought I was dying because I had pushed all my insides out. But worse was to come. My little Shane was struggling to breathe and he died after a very short time while I was holding him in my arms. I couldn't stop crying, thinking I had killed him by the force of my pushing. As I got more and more hysterical, the doctors became concerned about me and had to sit down and explain to me that this was not the case. They told me that I had a rare blood group—O negative—and that sometimes babies in this situation are delivered stillborn or only live for a short time. When I had calmed down and accepted that the baby's death had not been my fault, I just thought to myself that maybe if there had been an incubator or if the doctor had come in time my baby boy would still be alive.

All this came as a big shock to everyone in the family and we were all numbed by the experience. But it affected my husband worst of all as he really wanted this baby. That night sleeping was impossible. I tried to control my tears but every time the screwed up little face of my baby whom I had held in my arms for such a very short time came into my mind, fresh floods of tears came. In the morning, very early while it was still dark, with the sky full of stars, I got down on my knees and prayed. Looking at the beautiful sky I chose the very biggest star for our family and decided that there must be a reason why Jesus took our child—but one day I knew we would meet little Shane again. I still had my faith even though I felt that my whole world had collapsed.

When I found out that I was pregnant again, my in-laws were overwhelmed with happiness at the news after the loss of my first child because this would be their first grandchild—and from their youngest child. My in-laws, the Jenkins', had decided that we should both now live with them. I left behind my parents, brothers and sister, so this was a very big step to take and full of disappointment for me. I felt as if something would be missing from my life, as the bond I had with my family was so strong. Still, I accepted that I had to grow up and find another way of life with this new family that I now had. On my arrival my in-laws were very happy and they received me graciously. I was made very welcome but they made it quite clear that their way of living was never going to change just to please me. They changed my name to Merriam, which was used by them only.

On the first morning in our new home with the Jenkins, Ighsan was able to help me to feel more at home but we were awakened by his mother who told us that breakfast was ready and that we had five minutes to get to the table. Breakfast was to be another ordeal for me. It was just a plain meal of fried egg, toast and tea but I was amazed to see that they ate with their fingers—just as my grandmother had done. I had felt sure that educated people like the Jenkins' would use knives and forks so I sat there at the table staring, not knowing what to do, until I could stand it no longer. I felt so embarrassed for them that I leapt up and started to search in the kitchen for knives and forks—even though I wasn't capable of using them, I felt I just had to try.

I quickly found out that I had a lot to learn and that my mother-in-law would be the one to teach me. She wanted to teach me how to cook a good curry and a lot of other things that I thought would be impossible to learn. I felt so afraid—especially as they always spoke their own language, which was Afrikaans because they were from Capetown in South Africa so I couldn't understand a word that was said. This made me feel so lonely and I knew that they would have liked me to learn to speak it. Another custom they had that made me feel very uneasy was that in the toilet there was a metal container for us to use to cleanse the bottom. I drew the line at this and totally refused to use it, insisting instead that Ighsan buy me some toilet paper.

During the day, I would prepare the supper with my mother-in-law who would repeatedly vow that she was going to make a good Muslim woman of me by the time she had finished. I would only see my husband in the evenings when I had finished all the meal preparation. All the different courses took a lot of time to prepare and used spices that I had never heard of. My mother-in-law took her teaching task very seriously and every day there was something new for me to learn. I think because of this I learned lots of really useful things that many women these days are not able to do—not just cooking, but also sewing, embroidery, knitting, crocheting and lots of things to show me how to look after a home properly and to always take care of your husband, fulfilling all his needs.

Then one morning the postman arrived with some mail and my mother-in-law handed me a letter that was addressed to Ighsan with a Government stamp on it. At first I did not think anything of this and just put it aside for my husband to read because he was out yet again looking for a job. In those days jobs were very difficult to find so he would often be out of the house looking for a job or, because most of the time he was unsuccessful and disappointed, he would spend time with his friends just hanging around. This would make me very cross as I thought he should spend more time with me.

Later that afternoon, as soon as he arrived home, I handed him the letter. He was so surprised and shocked as he read it that I knew something was seriously wrong. My hands shook as I read the letter. I was not expecting to read this sort of news at all. My husband was being called up for military training and would have to go and stay at the barracks. As I read this I just broke down into floods of tears. I wondered who would look after me now and love me the way he did. I was so afraid but all Ighsan said was that at least he would be earning a salary in the army and so he would be able to support me and not have to depend on his parents any longer. He looked a little excited, yet sad at the same time. That night I clung to him, afraid to let him go. I could already feel the loneliness that lay ahead as I thought about him leaving me in a few weeks time.

Although I was now a married woman, I was still very young and I missed my parents and family. I used to cry so much for my parents that my mother-in-law would get worried. She thought I would run away to see them, as I was not allowed to see them without my husband's permission even though they lived close by. Her solution was to put me in bed with her and her husband. I would find this so embarrassing that I would lie awake, holding back my tears until I was sure that they were asleep then sneak off back to my room in the middle of the night. This happened so often that I eventually realised that crying would get me nowhere except my mother-in-law's bed, which petrified me, so I became even more determined to hide my feelings.

I remember an occasion when Ighsan was away that I was invited to a cousin's wedding. I was so excited that I would see my parents and I really looked forward to it. My parents-in-law accompanied me and, despite my wanting to stay and talk with my parents, whom I had not seen for some time, they insisted I go home with them after just two hours at the reception. My mother-in-law said she had to 'look after her son's property'. I was amazed and upset at this and went and hid in the toilets, hoping they would not find me. Needless to say, my mother-in-law soon discovered my hiding place, knocked on the door of the cubicle, took my hand and escorted me out of the hall. We drove home in silence, with me crying the whole way for my parents and when we got home she undressed me, put me in my bedclothes and tucked me nicely in her bed. I fell asleep crying. There were many things that I truly disliked about living with my in-laws—these are just some of them—and I just lived for Ighsan to return from the army when my whole body and soul would light up with joy.

The next few months flew by so fast. I was so excited about having another baby that it even helped me not to miss my husband too much. When I was about five months pregnant my husband came home on a weekend pass and he was so excited to find out that his parents had bought him a small motorbike. This was for him to learn how to use instead of a car because petrol was so expensive in Rhodesia and this bike he would use for work when he came out of the army. With the little bit of knowledge that he had on how to ride a motorbike, he asked me to sit at the back and he said he would take me—with my big stomach—for a ride. He reassured me that he would be very careful because I was pregnant. We went out on the road with me sitting on the back of the bike, clinging on for dear life because he was going at such a speed in full traffic. I think maybe he had taken some alcohol or something, because he just carried on pressing the accelerator and going faster and faster, ignoring my fear. When he reached a corner, he shouted to me 'Watch how I take this corner!' The next thing I knew I was flying into the air with my hands on my stomach. When I landed and realised what had happened, I found that I had badly bruised my knees and my forehead had a big cut on it. A kind passer-by had to phone for an ambulance and we were both rushed to the hospital. We weren't unconscious but we were very badly hurt and I had to be admitted to hospital to receive treatment because the baby in my stomach was threatening to come out before its time. That night I just lay there looking at the ceiling wondering why I had to listen to my husband all the time. I knew that I was also to blame and that I could have lost my baby because of negligence so, once again, I just cried myself to sleep. I remained in the hospital for about two weeks; then, when the doctor released me, I was told 'no more motorbike racing' because the next time I would really lose my baby. From what I can remember my husband never said sorry to me.

When he was away, I missed my husband so badly that I jumped at the chance to go to the army camp at the King George VI Barracks in Salisbury (Known as KG6), where he was undergoing his basic training, to see him. He had phoned me to come to the camp and I just caught the next bus to the barracks without knowing what it would involve. He told me to go around to the back and he would get me into the camp. I looked up at the fence in amazement—it must have been over twelve feet high and topped with barbed wire—but he came along with some of his army buddies and they threw a blanket over the top of the fence and I scrambled over with their help. I brushed myself down and managed to ignore the many cuts and bruises I had gained in the process. I was so excited that I never gave a thought to the fact that I was doing anything wrong or that if I had been caught I could have been shot by a sentry. This was just another of the things—dreams and adventures—that I did for love. This dream soon turned into a nightmare when the Military Police burst in as I slept in my husband's arms. We were both escorted to the main guardroom for questioning. Eventually I was released with a warning not to try anything like that again. Ighsan didn't get off quite so lightly as he had to attend a court martial for his actions. He was subsequently denied a pass for two whole months. He couldn't come home and see me during this time and it felt like a lifetime.

My baby son was born in December 1971 just before midnight, at the Lady Chancellor Maternity Home in Salisbury. One vivid memory of my time in labour was hearing a song that was being played in the nurses' room. As I pushed and pushed, I could hear 'Raindrops keep falling on my head' by Sacha Distel and this song made me feel so happy and proud. But there were a lot of complications with the birth—they had to pull him out with some forceps and his little head had lumps all over it. Despite this traumatic entry into the world, he was a very healthy little guy with long black hair—so long that he looked like a little Eskimo. He quickly put on weight and his lumps gradually disappeared. All this brought so much confidence and happiness to the family that it helped us all to come to terms with the death of the little baby boy I had lost not long ago. We named this new baby Shane in his honour.

Shane at 7 months

Returning to my parents-in-law's home with my baby was difficult because my mother-in-law would not let me even change or wash my baby because she was so afraid that I would drop the baby or something. She even went as far as choosing the baby clothes for him to wear. Being cut out of my baby's life like this really hurt me so that, at times, crying was my only solution. My mother-in-law would then tell me to grow up. She just didn't seem to appreciate what she was doing to me and, of course, just after the birth I was in a delicate state anyway. This thoughtless behaviour continued when she told me that I was forbidden to see my family, explaining that I had to wait for my husband's permission. When Ighsan arrived home on leave again, he was so excited that he had a son and he was keen for us to have our own house, our own little family home, but we had to stay with his parents for the time being.

When my son was about four months old I found out that another baby was on the way. This was so exciting for us both that when I told my husband (who was now back in the army) he asked for special leave and immediately looked for accommodation for us. We managed to find a cheap, small house with just two rooms. This was like heaven to me. I scrubbed the place and kept it looking like home. I enjoyed being the little housewife. The only time I didn't like my new home was at nighttime. At night I always felt afraid that someone would break in. I tried to ignore the loneliness and would always talk to my son, pretending there were a lot of people in the house.

My life alone was filled with worry for my husband because he was a soldier in the Rhodesian army. Things had got really bad and many soldiers were being killed in the area where Ighsan was posted. At this time they also started calling up the older men, so my father who was in his forties had to do military service as well, leaving my mother alone too. This made things worse.

When Ighsan came home on leave or a weekend pass, he would always bring me a present—chocolates, flowers, jewellery, etc. One time he brought me a small sealed box. I opened it to discover that it was a vinyl record (a single—we called it a '45' in those days) that he said he had listened to while he was out in the bush. It was 'Close to You' by the Carpenters—a beautiful song that still rings in my brain to this day. Of course, I played this over and over again when my husband was away in the war and it was such a comfort to me that I can never forget it. Her told me that it reminded him of me and that all he had to do was look at the beautiful birds in the bush and he would know that I would always be there for him—his beautiful bride. That night, as we lay in bed, he promised me that if anything should happen to him while out in the bush, his spirit would never die. It would always be close to me, looking after me. This brought tears to my eyes but they were not tears of pain or sadness but tears of true love.

Cross-border incursions by the two main guerrilla groups operating against the country (Joshua Nkomo's Zimbabwe African People's Union—ZAPU—operating from Zambia and Robert Mugabe's Zimbabwe African National Union—ZANU—operating from Mozambique) aroused fears and great tension in the white population of Rhodesia.

I was continually thinking that my father, husband or brothers could be killed in the war. My two brothers, Harold and Kenny, had also been called up into the army and they were sent to a very dangerous post in a little town called Binga in north-western Rhodesia, where lots of the soldiers were losing their lives. My brothers were so young—just out of high school. When my husband was made up to sergeant, he was also transferred to Binga and so now they were all serving together in this highly dangerous place in the same regiment—the Rhodesia Defence Regiment. But at least they could try to protect one another while they were fighting for their lives. During this time, Harold, who loved animals so much, found a baby monkey and called her Judy. He looked after this monkey as if it was a child and he taught it to behave like a human being. She liked eating the same food that the soldiers ate and she stayed with Harold wherever he went. When he was given a pass to go home on leave, he took Judy home with him to my mother. She was such a loving little pet that everyone loved to play with her and she slept just like a baby in a little cot that my brother had made for her. As Judy got older, she no longer liked to be near women or young girls and would only be close to men or boys. She acted as though she was in love with my father—her face showing her happiness whenever she saw him. My mother became so cross with Judy's behaviour that she eventually gave her away. As she left, Judy cried and made funny little noises as though she was refusing to go.

During my pregnancy with this baby, I don't know why but I felt like this was to be a very special baby. The baby in my stomach kicked so gently that I just knew it was going to be a little girl and sent to me from heaven. She seemed to me to be just like my shiny star in the sky. The big day arrived early in 1973 when I delivered a beautiful baby girl, the sweetest little angel I've ever seen. She had a full mop of jet-black hair and a face that just brought a smile. With tears of love in my eyes, I nicknamed her Sunshine, and called her Aida after the famous opera by the Italian composer Giuseppe Verdi. The feeling of love was so overwhelming that I protected my little Sunshine from everything. No one was to even breathe on her, as I was always afraid she would get ill. I truly loved my new daughter and am ashamed to say that I didn't take as much notice of my son as I should. I could never explain why this was. I loved them both but felt that I had to protect little Sunshine, simply knowing that there was something magical about her.

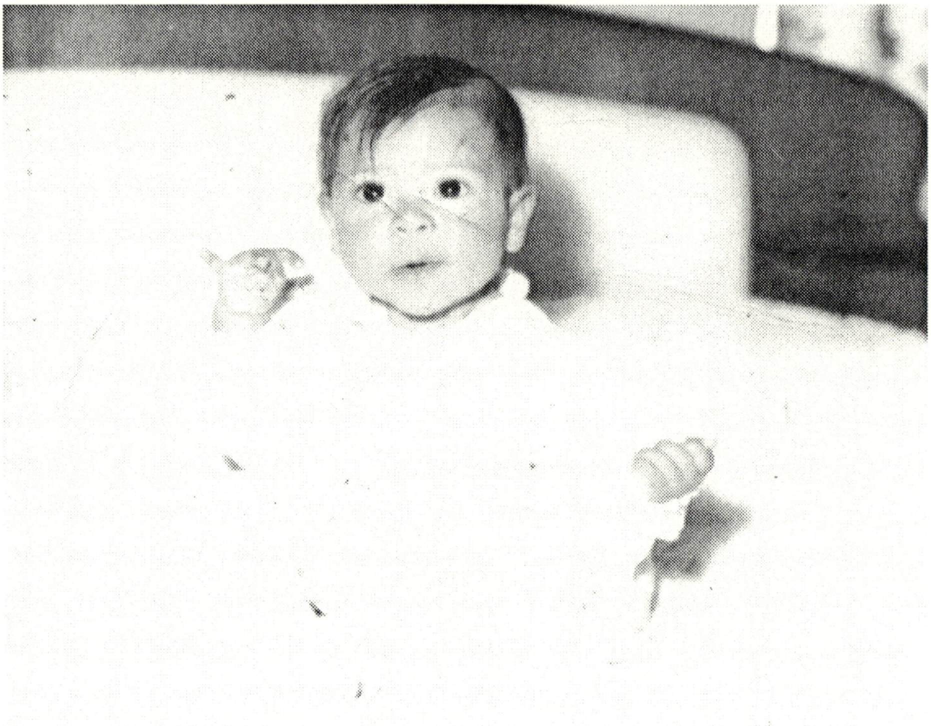

My Sunshine—Aida

Aida on a tricycle

Aida

6

Separation

Sanctions and increased guerrilla activity had forced the Smith regime into an agreement (brokered by the British Government) to hold free elections in February 1980. Robert Mugabe and his ZANU party won a landslide victory at the polls. On the 18th April 1980, the Republic of Zimbabwe came into being with Mugabe as Prime Minister. This made me so happy because the fighting had come to an end and my husband, father and brothers would soon be discharged from the army—they would be safe and coming home!

When my husband did come home from the army, he found a job working for a large bakery as an apprentice confectioner. The money he was paid was not much but we managed in our little house that was almost empty. Both of our children had grown so beautiful. You could see the happiness shining from their little faces but with my little daughter, Sunshine, it was very difficult to explain, but I felt that there was always something extra special. I was continually afraid of her crying too much or hurting herself so I would be by her side all the time just protecting her with all my love, afraid that if I let go she would be taken away from me. Just before Aida was due to start school she was running to buy an ice cream when she ran in front of an ice cream bicycle cart and suffered head injuries. She went into hospital and was kept there for about three months. Soon after she came out of the hospital she developed lumps behind her ears on occasions, which could only be treated with antibiotics. The doctors could never explain why these lumps appeared. Despite these difficulties she was such a cute child. She spoke only in a sort of baby language and even when it was time for her to go to school she didn't want to speak properly. Eventually, the school had to write me a letter asking me to speak to my child properly.

Shane and Aida

My husband became qualified and got a better job as a work foreman with a very good salary and also benefits such as free housing and schooling for the children. This job was in a place called Mutare, a little town about three hundred miles away from all our family, on the border with Mozambique. We got a house with three bedrooms and I was so proud of my new home. My husband didn't want me to do any work in the house so he hired someone to handle all the chores that needed doing and I had lots of time for the children and myself. Once again I had a feeling of happiness and contentment. I took up a course of rabbit breeding—something I had always liked to do in my spare time. What I didn't know at this time was that while my husband had so much, he still wanted more—like having girlfriends at his workplace and going out at night. He would always say that he was working overtime because he was the foreman, but the thing is that he could never manage to be very tidy as he always left telltale traces around the house and the car about his secret lifestyle. I would often find condoms—both used and unused—under the seat of the car, semen stains on his clothing, ladies' hairclips and bracelets and sometimes a blanket in the car. Whenever I caught him out he would always say that it wouldn't happen again. This worry and stress began to affect my everyday life with the children and I was becoming so miserable that eventually I planned to take my two children to stay with my family in Harare. I knew that I had to choose a night when he wasn't at home. I packed what few belongings I could carry for both my children and myself and decided to make my way to the railway station. I had no means of transport so I had to walk. The shortcut I took meant that I had to cross the Mutare River, holding the suitcase and my two children. This was a real struggle and we slipped under the water but eventually managed to climb out the other side and, of course, by the time we arrived at the railway station we were soaking wet. We then caught a train to Harare. We stayed for a short while with my family but eventually I managed to get my own place in town—a small two-bedroomed flat. I also found a job in the courthouse doing filing and typing. The salary was good enough to cover my rent and food and I also claimed maintenance for my two children, so we were once again happy and contented. But I was soon battling again when my in-laws tried to get custody of my children. They just refused to let go and hired a lawyer to say that I was not a fit mother; this misfired for them, however, as this lawyer found that I was an excellent mother. They lost their case after a long battle. But the struggle still wasn't over for me.

A few weeks later there was knock on my door and when I opened it, there stood my husband, holding a gun in his hand. It was one of those guns they give you in the army called an F.N.—a semi automatic rifle with a twenty round magazine. I was terrified for myself and for my children! He forced his way into my house, took me to the bathroom, calling the two children to follow us. He closed the door behind them and we all started crying and begging him please to put the gun away. Despite our tears and panic and his children being so upset, he refused, saying that today he was going to kill all of us, starting with me and killing himself last. The reason he gave was that if we could not live together as a family, then we would die together because he couldn't live without us. He certainly looked a mess—his eyes were bright red, he was crying and sweating heavily. He commanded us to pray and all three of us got on our knees, with the children screaming and holding on to his legs begging him to stop. I tried telling him that we could talk and that I would take him back and we would live together again as husband and wife but nothing I said would make him change his mind. Luckily our screams were heard by a passing neighbour who immediately reported the disturbance to the police. Within a few minutes the police arrived, breaking down the door as we cowered in the bathroom. They arrested my husband and took him away but when it was time for me to press charges I refused. It turned out that he was not in a lot of trouble and he was only given a prison sentence of six months for the offence of possessing a firearm.

After a few months I went back to my husband and once again we lived in Mutare. I had thought long and hard about going back to him. The gun incident had made me realise how important the children and I were to him and I felt sorry for him. I thought I would do everything I could to make this marriage work out for the children's sake because now he had stopped drinking and smoking. He was being such a good husband that I soon forgot the past and we started to rebuild our marriage with plenty of love.

For a while our lives were happy and settled. The war had ended and we were back together as a family, with my husband in a good job. But this was not to last. After a while the new Government started to make a lot of changes and many firms were closing down, our money was becoming devalued and the cost of living soared. Life became so hard. Eventually my husband was put out of work and given a small pension. He got another job—just a temporary one as that was all he could get—but in this process he started drinking and having lots of girlfriends. Our lives were falling apart yet again. The happiness we had had simply vanished and it made me very sad. My daily life became pure suffering because of the economic situation and with all the abuse my husband gave me. Finding out I was pregnant made matters worse and this time he was violent towards me. One day when I was just nine months pregnant he came home drunk and abusive. He hit me so badly that I was rushed to hospital. When I was admitted, I was so badly bruised that the doctor wanted to inform the police—but once again I refused to press charges against my husband. My baby son (who was to be named Marvin) only lived for one day and we buried him in Mutare. The day of the funeral I looked a sight with blue marks all over my face and body. I wept as I carried my little son's tiny white coffin. Once again I was crying all alone. Not even my family or his knew that our child had died as we had kept everything from them from the start of the pregnancy. We felt that we couldn't tell our families about any of our problems or about the pregnancy because they were all tired of the trouble we brought them and they thought it would be better if we divorced for the children's sakes. I just knew that this would be the end for us now. I felt I really hated my husband and refused to let him hold the coffin. I alone put my baby into the grave and all Ighsan could do was stand there by the grave as if he were frozen but with tears rolling down his face.

The following day I took both my children and caught the train back to Harare, to my family, without telling anybody what had happened.

Ighsan travelled to Harare separately and stayed with his family. At this point I thought divorce was the only solution and so we got a painful divorce. I felt devastated because, despite everything that had happened, he was my first love and the father of my two children. I watched as Ighsan started his new life in Harare. He began going out drinking, smoking cannabis and mixing with the wrong people. One night he was involved in a car accident that resulted in the deaths of two brothers who were his friends. After this he decided to make a new life for himself in the town of Masvingo. There he soon reverted back to the lifestyle he had had in Harare and was fired from his job. He returned to his family in Harare in shame.

Now that he was living close by again, Ighsan begged me to go back to him. He even resorted to arranging the intervention of my priest, Father Thomas, as he knew that he was the only man who could help him get us back together again. Eventually, Ighsan got back into my life once again and he moved into our family home. This time, though, I really felt that things had changed and he finally started to act like a loving 'husband' and a father to our children.

He was desperate to get work and with Jesus' help one of his applications was successful. The company needed a qualified confectioner in Blantyre in Malawi—a landlocked country to the north east of Zimbabwe—and they were willing to send the plane ticket for Ighsan. It would only take three hours to get there by plane and we were so desperate that he left alone the following week, saying that once he was settled he would send for us. Meanwhile, I managed to find a job as a typist with a good salary that enabled me to get a small house and pay for our living expenses including someone to help with the children. I really enjoyed my job and made lots of new friends. In my spare time I started to sew. I bought a sewing machine, hired another girl and started sewing dresses for people who could not afford to buy in the shops. When I had saved up some money, I also bought a knitting machine very cheaply from a white lady who was leaving the country and then I paid somebody to teach me to use the machine. I made lots of jerseys every week and so with the money from this and my small sewing business, I was now making quite a lot of money. The children and I moved into a bigger place with more rooms and even a small swimming pool for the children—they had everything any child could dream of. The support from my ex-husband continued but there was no news of him finding us a place for us to be together.

During this time my family had all moved to my father's plot in Gweru. After a while I told my children we were going on a holiday to visit their grandma in Gweru, where there was a beautiful plot for them to play and maybe my son could go fishing and hunting with his uncles. The children thought this was a great adventure. My father had started gold mining with his sons and, using his past experience, he built himself a gold crusher, which ran on petrol, not electricity. Another way to catch the gold is with cyanide and he also built tanks to do this. He was doing very well with the gold business and running the plot at the same time. We prepared for our holiday in Gweru by giving all our workers leave while I took a month off, locked our house and caught the most expensive bus with my excited children for our first holiday together. Our journey went quickly—we travelled over four hundred miles but didn't feel tired on arrival. When we got off the bus a beautiful sight met my eyes—my father was there to meet us at the bus stop to take us home. Everybody, including my grandmother, was at home waiting for us and it struck me just how important it is to have a family still alive. I treasure every moment of happiness because, believe me, it passes by so fast. It's just like a dream that you wish you could hold on to forever.

When my one-month's holiday was up I was totally relaxed. My children had had a wonderful time and I felt peace of mind knowing Ighsan would send for me when he was ready, so I had not a care in the world. Yet again my happiness wasn't to last. We arrived home feeling tired from the journey but happy to be home, but when I opened the door and looked into the house we saw that everything had gone! There wasn't a thing in any of the rooms. I was in total shock, with no idea how we were going to manage. I ran straight to the police but they were of no help. All they said was that they thought it was an inside job done by maybe one of my workers. I was so upset, thinking why does all this happen to me? Just when my spirits are high something always has to happen to bring me crashing down. That night and for the next few nights we slept in a bed and breakfast place while I tried to find out what had happened but I had no luck—there was no trace of anything. All my lovely expensive things that I had worked so hard for had gone. All I could think of to do was to leave and go back to my parents to stay until my ex-husband sent for us.

The following day I put my notice in at work and left for Gweru with no belongings—just my two beautiful children and a few clothes. I was in despair and even started to wonder why I should worry about these earthly things when one day I will have complete fulfilment in my heavenly home. I left my life in Harare with tears of sadness running down my cheeks, trying hard not to show my children. I could see they were very hurt but I had to try to make them see that what we were doing was a new start to our lives and also would mean that we were near to my family, which was very important to us all.

I continued to wait for word from my ex-husband and I truly believed that we could make a new start but it was during this time that I heard that Ighsan had married one of his friends from high school called Amanda. As I recall, she looked just like me. He never told me even though he still phoned to speak to his children and still tried to come back into our lives. On a few occasions he came down to see us and the love would once again fall into place. We just seemed right together. I just stored my painful thoughts about him being married to someone else into the back of my head and tried to forget.

Life was not easy living with my family at this time. My parents were now living on their plot where we had recently visited for a holiday but they soon decided to move out of the plot into a small town house and have the plot done up properly to sell it one day. My father wanted to build a house by the mine and stay there as he thought that the war was over and also that he would be able to protect his machinery and all the things he had built through hard work and sweat. This mine was now his only means of survival for his sons and himself. The situation in the country was rapidly getting worse. Many firms closed down and people found it difficult to get any jobs. The family's new house only had three bedrooms and we were all squashed together so I tried hard to find a job that would enable me to get a place of my own with the children. I made a desperate search for a job and got one with the help of a white lady who got me into the government health department working as a clerk that included typing and filing. I then managed to get a small flat near my work where there was a school for the children. At first, working, as a person of mixed race, for the health department was very unpleasant because none of the other African girls wanted to talk to me and they gossiped about me in their African language. They had no idea that I had grown up with an African granny so I understood every word they said. One day, I'd had enough and they all got a shock when I answered them back in Shona. From then on life at work became a bit easier and we all became friends eventually. I think they probably felt sorry for me.

I worked hard and was a good mother to my precious children who I loved more than anything in this whole world. I made sure that they had all the things they needed and I was always working. In my spare time, from morning until late at night I would do whatever crossed my mind to earn a bit extra. I was always full of business ideas; I just wasn't a woman who would sit down waiting for things to happen. While I was strong and fit, work must be done.

Although we managed well as a family, I didn't always feel secure living alone with my children. One day there was a knock on the door and standing there were two undercover police saying I should come to the police station for questioning. When we arrived at the station I was put in a small room with one of the gentlemen. He sat very close to me and asked me if I had bought some stolen candles. My immediate reply was 'why should I buy candles when we use electricity?' He then came even closer, until our lips were just touching and when he spoke to me his spit splashed all over my face. This made me feel intimidated and abused but I could do nothing about it. I simply sat there and cried. After some hours they told me to go home and I never heard about this incident again. I think they only did this because they somehow knew that there was no man at home with me so they could easily get away with it. I just knew then that this kind of racial abuse to innocent people would never end.

A few years passed and still my ex-husband continued to send us money but no news about us going to stay with him. Sometimes I thought he just felt sorry for me and that's why he sent money. I was filled with worry and doubt about my future and all my hopes and dreams were slowly disappearing. This situation carried on for almost another year, until one day at work I received some plane tickets from him for the following week. I was so happy. I immediately put my notice in to leave and started to sell some of my things but was stopped in my tracks when I got a phone call at work from my mother-in-law to tell me that Ighsan had had an accident and was in a coma. He was being transferred by plane to Harare Hospital, Zimbabwe, where there were more facilities to treat his injuries. I went, in a split second, from being full of hope and happiness to being consumed by worry and pain. I prepared in a haze of unhappiness to leave for Harare from Gweru but then I received yet another phone call from my mother-in-law. This time she had even worse news. She told me that Ighsan had just passed away. I barely heard her as she continued. They had organised for me and the children to be brought to where the funeral was to take place. I couldn't take it all in. We had come so close to being reunited; just one more week to go before I could have gone to be with the only man I had ever loved, the father of my children.

As the news began to sink in I started to wonder to myself where was he going to at that time of the night? I thought maybe he was just so happy to have me and the children going out to join him that he was out celebrating. I caught the lift that my parents-in-law had organised with my two children and on the way I had to explain to them that we were going to their father. I told them that he was in hospital and that he had had an accident with his car and had passed away. I later learned that when Ighsan had the accident, he was on his way home from a pub and not wearing a seat belt when the car crashed into the huge clock tower in the centre of Blantyre. He sustained injuries across his forehead and was taken to hospital in a coma. His parents had made arrangements for him to be rushed by plane from Malawi to Parirenyatwa Hospital in Harare where he only lived for a day before dying in his sleep. All I saw now was the pain in my children who truly loved their father. As I looked at my two children crying and struggling to understand what I had just told them, I was reminded of the time when he had held us captive in the bathroom and they had begged him not to kill them. This only showed me how they truly loved their father. Little Sunshine clung to me with her tiny hands, asking me why it had happened and I really didn't know what to say. I asked my Jesus why me, always me? I prayed for him to give me some answers. None came. All I did was just sit there like I was lost in space, feeling like a dead person.

The journey took ages and I prayed the whole way. When we arrived at the hospital we found someone waiting for us with a message. They said that everyone was already at the cemetery, because Muslims had to be buried the same day before sunset. Hearing this news my children cried so much but I could only choke with shock. When we arrived at the place where he had been laid out on a table after his brothers had bathed him, he looked so much alive with his long black hair and a moustache, that my heart almost stopped beating. I screamed his name over and over and my tears splashed all over his face. I tried desperately to awaken him and still tried to kiss him the way I knew how, because he always told me he would die without my tiger juice. I just couldn't say goodbye to my first love.

In the fog of my grief I slowly realised that the other woman crying and standing by his side was his other wife Amanda. This was the biggest shock for me. I just did not know what to do when she came over and hugged me. We were both crying for our 'husband' but all the way home this really pained me so much. I knew that with his religious background (he was always in the mosque, praying every Friday) he must have been in absolute torment, not knowing what he was going to do with two 'wives' which he loved very much. I learnt later that he also had two children with this woman but that she had left him because she knew that he would never let go of his past with me and my children. This was—and still is—so acutely painful to me that I never wanted to mention all this in my story. I just wanted to store it all away and try to forget it but I decided to write about it because to this day I have never stopped thinking about my first love. He will always remain in my heart and wherever he is I will always be with him.

After the funeral I decided to go straight home to my little flat with my children. I could not bear to spend another day in Harare, so I left immediately and felt that I was on the journey to hell. All the way home I cried and prayed, holding on to my little Sunshine and my son, nicknamed Papa. But this time praying was not the answer. I was in despair as I realised that everything goes so badly for me and wondered why. Sometimes these things only happen to good people because the devil wants to change your good way of thinking, making you evil. When he knows he's got you, only then is he satisfied.

7

New Life, New Relationship

I went back to work after a long rest of one month but it was very difficult to be happy and to act as though everything was normal and my thoughts were always on my children. I felt that everybody at work only pretended to like me and I just had to push myself to keep working. Even if a person tried to joke with me I felt like crying instead of laughing.

My sister Wendy, who lived in South Africa, decided she would take the risk of returning to Zimbabwe for a visit, leaving behind her husband and two children, as they would be at greater risk than her. This was because a few years earlier some relative had made false allegations to the police about her husband, Brian. He was accused of smuggling goods into Zimbabwe. As a white man, he was arrested and put straight into prison. When we eventually found out which prison he was being held in, bail was arranged for him and while he was out on bail the whole family were forced to leave the country and flee to South Africa. Their escape was carefully planned and the two children were playing in the garden—with no shoes and with uncombed hair—when they were suddenly collected and bundled onto a plane bound for South Africa. The day after Wendy and her family had left, that same relative who had made the accusations hired a big truck and completely emptied their house of all its contents—even including the pot plants—and then also emptied Brian's computer shop of its contents. She came back to Zimbabwe just to see her loved ones and brought with her many gifts, which included some special whisky for her two brothers Harold and Kenny who had survived the war and also her precious father who also liked a drink now and again.

With all the excitement in the home we decided to celebrate with my brothers and sister by having a drink of whisky and then, for a change, we went out to the local pub, where we met some of my brothers' old army buddies. My sister did not stay long as she had to leave and get some sleep for a rushed trip by train the next day back to South Africa. I don't really know why I remained with my brothers but I did and from what I remember I was only drinking some coke at the time, but my brothers were both looking for girls. The next thing I knew it was the next morning. I got up off my mother's large sofa with my clothes in a heap on the floor beside me, and a painful headache, wondering why my clothing was on the floor and feeling like I was drugged.

After my sister left everything went back to normal and the weeks just flew past, but without getting my period. I thought maybe I had malaria because I was always feeling tired and just wanted to sleep all the time. I made an appointment with the family doctor and he confirmed that another baby was on its way. I had to believe the doctor but I just didn't understand it. This was a terrible shock to my mind, as I knew there was nothing I did with anybody. Looking back desperately on that evening in the pub with my brothers, I came to the conclusion that one of my brothers' army buddies must have put something into my drink and raped me while I was asleep in my mother's house. I never told anybody and just kept it as one of my many secrets. My mother eventually guessed the truth—only that I was pregnant and nothing else. Every time she asked I would start crying so she eventually stopped asking, knowing that there must have been something very painful for me.

This was the loneliest time of my life; it was just passing me by. This secret of mine made me feel so ashamed and dirty and I thought I would have to carry my secret with me to my grave. This is why I did not, could not, tell my mother at the time but I feel now that I can—and must—write about my secret.

I racked my brain for clues about who the man who raped me might be and I started asking veiled questions of my brothers and their friends. Gweru being such a small town, all the gossip pointed to one man. It was a man called George who was hated and feared by everyone. He had once been in jail for shooting his wife through the head with his army-issue FN rifle, leaving behind four young children. When I realised this was the man responsible for my predicament, I knew that I could not tell anybody at all. I feared for my life as I thought that he might just kill me and my family if I got him in any more trouble. Knowing who had done this to me did not make things any easier. I still felt so dirty and hated myself for what had happened to me. As I walked around the small farm town where we lived and where everyone knew one another, I was constantly looking out for him and trying to avoid him. My life was totally miserable at this point but, even so, I felt some excitement at the prospect of a new life. This baby was going to come into this world no matter what and would be all mine to love and cherish.

I was almost eight months pregnant when I started getting contraction pains, knowing it was too soon. I had to inform my mother who collected me and rushed me to Birchenough Maternity Hospital in Gweru. Giving birth was not a problem and the labour was very short and painless so that almost as soon as I arrived at the hospital, I gave birth to the most beautiful dark little baby girl—who looked like a doll—on 10th June 1981. She shared her birthday with my mother, who named her after herself—Jane. She was almost three pounds in weight and as she was premature she had to be put into an incubator. She was fed by a long tube through her nostrils. She now had to fight for her own survival without me to help my precious baby.

With all the delight and happiness I felt after the birth, my mother came to me and simply said she could not plait African hair. She said nothing else about the baby's appearance or who her father might have been. I supposed she had guessed what had really happened to me but was hoping for me to tell her the truth about my little baby but I just decided to just keep all this my own secret.

Looking at and loving my beautiful baby, I did not feel I was raped at all. When I took her home after she was finally discharged from the hospital, my children were so happy to meet their little sister who was so tiny. They nicknamed her 'Nippy'. As she grew I think we all spoiled Nippy the most because she was always so delicate and small with a different complexion to the rest of my children. I didn't want her to grow up thinking she was any different from the rest and also I knew that I couldn't forget my other children—especially little Sunshine. When I went back to work after all the strain of nearly losing my baby it was hard but I did manage and my only priority was to make sure that nothing was ever going to split up my little nest. I kept going just to protect and guide my children.

Life settled down at home (Shane at this time was taking Shotokan karate lessons and was soon entering competitions) and Jane was adored by all the family and given extra attention by my daughter Aida, who so truly loved her sister that Jane grew up thinking that Aida was her mother—I was called by my first name. These two pretty girls would dress the same and even went as far as sleeping in the same bed. On Sundays, Aida always got up first thing in the morning to prepare their clothing for church, which was something she did all on her own. The bond between the two was something not even I could understand but also which you could not interfere with—it was just so right. Jane was growing up with a good little 'mother'.

At this time I worked with a lot of doctors and one day I was introduced to an Australian expatriate English teacher by the name of Dave who taught at the local school. He was also my son Shane's English teacher. Even during our very first meeting I could tell that there was something so special about Dave and he must have felt the same way about me too, because the following day he was back at my office to invite me to supper. For the next few weeks we enjoyed each other's company and started to become very close. Later that year he moved in with me. This helped with my bills and he also helped me by looking after the children, who really loved him. His favourite was always Sunshine and they got on like a house on fire, him being an English teacher and Aida being so clever in English which meant they always had something in common. She would go and watch him play football and they would do the grocery shopping together at the weekend. They had bonded like father and daughter. Despite this newfound happiness, never did I forget my ex-husband who was my first love and in my thoughts and prayers for the rest of my life.

Just as life was beginning to get better and more settled, yet again a sudden shock hit us all. My grandmother Jessie was diagnosed with cancer in her legs and she also had problems eating. By this time she was living with her daughter (my auntie Margaret) who lived in Bulawayo so that she could be looked after. My grandmother had always been such a stubborn woman so she didn't make it easy for her daughter to help her. Even though she was very ill, she wanted to sleep and recover in the servants' quarters and, refusing a nice bed, simply insisted on just a blanket on the floor and a pillow off her own bed. She just lay there on the hard floor, not speaking much to anybody as if she already knew what was happening to her.

One morning during this short period of illness she was found dead by her daughter. This was so sad for all the family, who knew now that they had to try to make arrangements for her burial, which would have to be in her tribe's trust land of Shurugwe where she had lived with her parents as a child. We who loved her were not allowed to go and bury her because things were dangerous in those areas for people who were of mixed race and also I don't think we were too welcome by some of the people. All I could do was just say a prayer in my heart, grateful that now she would be free of pain. It was a goodbye to the bravest, proudest woman I have ever known and whom I loved with all my heart—my first 'mother'.

While I was still grieving for my grandmother, my boyfriend asked me to go on holiday to Malawi with him for a rest. After some thought, we packed our bags and left the children with my mother. Leaving my children behind—even for just one month—was the hardest thing to do, but also getting to know my boyfriend (who had recently asked me to marry him) was important too so I felt I had to go. Our holiday in Malawi was so beautiful in so many ways. We travelled by bus to each town, just enjoying the towns and meeting lovely people who were so poor. They were very proud of everything they owned and it gave them great joy to share whatever little they had. One little village we passed through on our journey, called Cape McClear, was the best place I've ever been to. It was situated near the seaside and we booked for the night in a small room. With romantic music playing in the background and a beautiful warm night, we decided to strip and play in the water. With the darkness and solitude this made the whole thing even more romantic and it led us to go further without taking any precautions. Of course, we thought that as this was our first mistake, nothing would happen and we left it at that. We had so much fun that not even in an entire lifetime could I explain how happy this man made me feel. With each and every time we kissed or made love, it was like a sharp knife paining me with love that brought tears to my eyes, leaving me speechless and weak. Each and every morning and evening we used to look forward to having a shower together, where we would take it in turns to soap each other's body. We would laugh and kiss, sometimes slipping on the soap and always playing like children. At the back of my mind, though, being in Malawi also made me feel guilty because this was where I was supposed to have joined Ighsan to start a new life.

On our arrival home from Malawi I resumed my responsibilities of caring for my children. I was making breakfast for my family but I had to stop as just the smell of onions sent me to the toilet feeling sick. My suspicions were confirmed when I went to the doctor and he diagnosed me pregnant. I told my boyfriend straight away and he was happy with the news so we started making our future plans for a new life for us all in Australia where we would marry.

When I was almost nine months pregnant we went out for supper to the local hotel near our house. We were sitting enjoying ourselves when in walked some of Mugabe's soldiers. The atmosphere in the room immediately changed. They announced that they were taking me with a lot of other women (mostly mixed race and white), saying we were prostitutes and needed to be sent to the rural areas to plough the lands and make an honest living. They repeatedly hit my boyfriend when he tried to stop them and he fell to the floor. I, along with the other women who had been enjoying their evening out, was dragged out of the hotel, leaving my boyfriend for dead. We were taken into a big open army truck with big bars to hold onto while standing up. It was nighttime—around eight in the evening—and the rain was pouring down so hard that we really had to hold on for our dear lives in the back of that truck. If we failed to listen to the soldiers, we would get a hiding with a wooden stick or a fist. We drove through the rain, while the soldiers who were in the back of the truck played with us, touching each and every part of us underneath our dresses. I was so terrified and afraid, especially when they caressed my stomach when they could see I was heavily pregnant. It was all a big joke to them.

We arrived at the old prison, which was situated in the centre of Gweru and the men shouted at us to get out. They prodded and pushed us as we scrambled down from the truck. In the pouring rain we had to run around the prison yard getting a good hiding as we ran and this made me urinate in my clothes. I knew I couldn't stop as I was too afraid to ask to use a toilet and if I hesitated I knew that I could have been trampled on by the other terrified women. I just kept moving as best I could, holding my stomach for dear life, trying to protect my unborn baby.

We were then herded like cattle into a second army truck and taken for miles on end to a second prison camp called Wa Wa prison outside the town. The soldiers were still enjoying doing abusive things to us all and the rain continued to pour down on us. Somehow the rain seemed to make matters even more unbearable. When we arrived at the second prison, we were herded out of the truck again with the soldiers poking their sticks at us and calling us prostitutes. We were put into some large foul-smelling cells. Once they had got us locked up, they told us to strip off our clothes because they were wet. It was then that I discovered that my feet were bare and they were swollen and covered in mud. I couldn't remember what had happened to my shoes. At this point we were thrown dirty, grey, smelly blankets, full of cockroaches. These were meant to cover us while we slept on the hard, cold floor, but I couldn't bring myself to touch it, as it was so filthy and smelly, so I refused to use it. I sat on the floor naked, trying to cover myself with my hands, shielding myself from the soldiers who just stood there laughing. I never slept the whole night, spending the time just crying and frozen to the core both with the cold in the prison and the icy terror I felt. I thought to myself that this was just a dream, a very bad dream. Surely nobody on earth could be this cruel to do this to somebody so innocent. One minute I had been sitting enjoying a meal, nine months pregnant, with my future husband; then, the next minute, without any explanation, I was being manhandled and taken to these disgusting conditions.

It seemed a long time before daylight came but in the morning we were given our clothes back in a large heap where all the women had to scramble to get their own things. We dressed as quickly as we could and then the soldiers herded us out to a very big open field where they had these huge iron dustbins of dry, rotten bread cut into gigantic slices and there were big metal mugs of black tea with no sugar. They shouted at us to eat, as we would need the strength. This terrified me even further and I broke down again. I was now also getting contraction pains and I thought all hope was gone, but my luck was about to change. By sheer good fortune, my boyfriend, Dave, had managed to find a good solicitor and brought him to the prison. They were now in the main office threatening to tell the world unless I was released. Being reunited with my boyfriend and family made me unbelievably happy. My son Shane was with them and as I staggered into the reception area he just looked at me with big swollen eyes through crying. My children and boyfriend had been convinced that I had died and while I was going through this terrible experience I was sure that I had left my boyfriend for dead and that my children would probably be taken into care if I couldn't get back to them. We hugged and cried together in front of the officials but then a fierce contraction reminded me that there were even more important things to do than hug my family. I didn't have time to wash before I was rushed to the Birchenough Maternity Hospital in Gweru. It was a complicated birth, with labour lasting two days but I finally produced a healthy baby girl. As I looked at this lovely baby and enjoyed holding her and keeping her close, I pushed everything that had been done to me to the back of my mind. I'm sure I would have gone mad if I had dwelled on the brutality of the soldiers, my fears that I would die and that my baby would be killed or the memories of holding my stomach to protect my baby as I was forced to comply with the soldiers' demands.

My mother was so happy for me and she nicknamed the baby 'Casper the friendly ghost', because she was so white with a thick mop of blonde hair. My new little girl was born in 1984 and named Rosalind after Dave's mother, but we all called her Rosie. Dave's mother and Rosie also shared the same birthday of 8th May.

Me at home pregnant with Rosie

Shane, Aida and Jane

8

More Sorrow

Just a few months after granny's death, my mother found a lump in her breast. It was examined and the doctor confirmed that it was cancer—the breast had to be removed at once. My mother's breast was removed but even after all that pain and suffering there was still more sadness to come. She was tested again and it was found that the cancer had spread. This time she would have to have treatment at the Mpilo Hospital in Bulawayo, which was about one hundred miles away from home. It was hoped that the treatment—radiotherapy—would keep her alive for some time. Each day she would leave Gweru at 6 a.m. on the bus and return late in the afternoon. From my office window at the Ministry of Health I would look out for her every afternoon as I knew what time she would be passing on her way back to my flat. I would stop working to look out for her. Seeing my mother walking past, looking frail, I had to choke back my tears knowing she didn't have long left to live. I could barely wait for 5 p.m. to come so that I could race home and see how my mother had got on.

She carried on with her course of treatment but was worried to find that it got worse each time she was subjected to the radiation. She eventually had to be admitted into hospital and I had never seen my mother so sad as she was on the day she went into the hospital. The deep sorrow was caused by a number of things. She had to leave her home but really didn't want to; she also had to leave her beloved husband and her youngest son Graham—her 'baby'. He was aged only nine at this time and my mother was very close to him. He had been born when she was in her late forties. And, of course, she was sad because she had had to accept that she was going to die. She knew that no one would be able to look after her son and love her family like she did.

Another thing that worried her as she prepared to die was that she had married many years ago in the registry court. This was not right in her eyes and now it was her dearest wish to get married in church with our Father Thomas officiating. She knew that her marriage would then be recognised by God. All the arrangements were quickly made and she married in church, sitting down on a comfortable chair with some cushions to hold her upright. To me this was a dream wedding because, after such a long time, I could see my mother was truly happy. She had what she wanted at last. The love for her family shone from her face as she married in church.

My mother after being diagnosed with cancer

After the ceremony and celebrations, my mother agreed without argument to go back to the hospital because things were not so good with her now. She became weaker by the day. The treatment my mother received at the hospital was awful. She suffered neglect on the ward—they did not comb her hair or wash and change her. When we visited her, she complained that nobody had fed her and the reason they gave her was that it was because she could not lift her arms or her body. Time went on and her condition deteriorated until eventually she could no longer tell us what was happening to her. It was heartbreaking to see this frail old lady lying helpless in her hospital bed and to see the scars in her scalp and on her body. We often found new scars and sometimes they looked like she had been lifted by someone with long nails. When the staff handled my mother, they must have done it in a really rough way as they left blue marks that stood out against her pale white skin. We couldn't ask her anything now because she could not talk—she just made sounds to show she needed something. When we asked should we call the nurse, she would start crying, kicking her legs to show she was terrified. I know now that some of the nurses ill-treated my mother and that this caused her illness to worsen. At the time it seemed there was nothing we could do to help her. She needed the treatments to save her life but she was being neglected and ill treated at the same time. This abuse upset me even more because I could see that it was racially motivated. Those nurses believed my mother to be a white woman. I do know there are a lot of black African people who are bigger racists than some of the white people. On one of my visits to see my mother, the pain of seeing her dying filled me with such emotion that I did not realize I was standing next to an electric bar heater and did not feel the pain from the fire. I later discovered that I had badly burned both of my legs. I couldn't think clearly about anything and I was focused solely upon my mother and willing her to get well.

My mother remained sick for one and half years, receiving radiotherapy in hospital. Just a few weeks before she died, she was told she could go home to spend a weekend with her family and she was taken to Bulawayo to her sister's place. This seemed like really good news to me, so I decided to catch the first bus out there to spend a weekend with my mother. I arrived late on the Friday night and when I saw my mother asleep in her bed she looked like there was absolutely nothing wrong with her. She was so peaceful. I got on my knees and kissed her gently on her face, then jumped into the bed beside her and fell into a deep sleep of relief, thinking maybe, since she was looking so well, things would change for the better. I thought—and hoped—that maybe the doctors had made a mistake. As morning came, I think we both awoke at just the same time. She was so happy to see me. I stayed on the edge of the bed to give her a cuddle and just that cuddle brought tears to my eyes because it was like cuddling a doll with no response from the other person. She was so weak that I could feel there was something terribly wrong. I felt dizzy with lots of emotions taking over my whole body. I just had to accept that my mother had not long to live. We talked about all sorts of things concerning the family and she was able to smile as we chatted. I just had to put on a big act because all I felt like doing was crying out as loud as possible. Maybe I could make someone out there hear me who could help my dear, beautiful mother whom I truly loved.

She hardly touched her breakfast and then she asked me to bathe her, so I helped to lift her out of the bed and we walked very slowly to the bathroom, which was just at the side of her room. After running the warm water, I undressed her and helped her into the bath. As I washed each and every inch of my mother's body I could not control the tears that poured down my face. It was so painful to see the body of the mother I loved so much. This was the only time I had realised that my mother had the most beautiful legs and that the scar from the operation for the removal of her breast looked so neat and well-healed like there was never anything wrong. I fell on my knees once again and kissed my mother. I told her that I loved her with all my heart. She was, as always, stronger than I was; she just told me not to cry and to be a big girl and look after the family, especially her baby Graham, aged nine. She did not even cry. She looked quite happy knowing that where she was going there would be no more pain. She gained strength too from her absolute belief in God. Helping my mother that day made me grow up in so many ways. This little woman, my mother, was going to leave me one day soon, taking something of me with her.

This realisation meant that I knew that I would have nobody in the world that would protect me any more. And I had regrets for the past as well as fear for the future. I just felt that when she was fit and well I could have given her much more time to love my children—her grandchildren—whom I had not wanted anybody but me to have. I just wanted to keep my children all to myself. I felt selfish and horrible and I should have given more love to my mother, but now, I knew, it was too late and I would always have to live with this painful experience in my heart until I die. The lesson I learned that day is that no matter how precious your children are to you, you should always share that joy with your family and then you would never be in the position of having to say you are sorry.

After my mother returned to the hospital I took my bus journey back home to Gweru and cried the whole way home, feeling empty and in some way blaming my Jesus for wanting to take my mother—the kindest, most loving person I had ever known who had truly loved people no matter what colour they were.

One weekend my mother made a special request of her sister Margaret. She asked her to phone us all at our homes back in Gweru and ask us—my father, my sister Wendy and me—to come immediately to the hospital in Bulawayo. As soon as we received this message we left, catching the first bus out. We were sure that the end had come but I do not understand how my mother knew. On arrival at the hospital, we stood around her bed looking down and talking to her with words of comfort. As we turned her in the bed to try to make her more comfortable, we saw that she had blue marks all over her body. As she saw us looking in dismay at the marks, she told us that she just wanted to be left alone on her pillow, just to look at us. She looked first at my father with tears running down her face, then at me and then at my sister Wendy. As we looked back at her we saw, through our own tears, that the whites of her eyes had suddenly turned yellow. Her tears became even worse—just pouring out of her like a tap, non-stop. Then suddenly her lungs started to make a rattling sound as she gasped for air. At about her fifth painful gasp like this she just remained there with her mouth open and this is when I realised that my mother had gone home to heaven. With this I started running towards some big windows at the hospital, intending to throw myself out, but I was caught by one of the nursing staff. They quickly gave me something to calm me down. I couldn't bear the thought that my mother had been tortured before she died because she couldn't do anything to help herself and because she was a white person. I have never seen or heard of any other person that died with tears running down their face.

When we started making funeral arrangements, it was such an embarrassing thing to find out that my father had no money for the casket. This was something where you could not ask for help outside the family, so I turned to my boyfriend and my sister's husband and all the arrangements were made. The day of the funeral was a nice, sunny day but no sooner had we begun to sing songs in church than it suddenly began to rain unexpectedly. When the priest was finished with his service and the coffin was being lowered into the grave, we found out that the grave had not been dug correctly and it was too small for the coffin to go into. My brothers Harold and Kenny had to take some spades and start digging in the pouring rain but still things did not work out straight away. After some time and lots of hard work, my two brothers finally got it right and, with a struggle, the coffin finally went into the grave. This seemed as though my mother was refusing to be buried. The burial service took almost two hours longer than expected.

After my mother was buried I just felt lost and empty. I had nobody to lean on to support me in my time of distress. I loved and missed her so dearly—my only best friend had gone. To this day I still think of the words she spoke to me before she died, when she was still able to speak. 'My darling daughter, you are my eldest and I really do know you have suffered in your life, but please promise me you will make something good with your life. No drinking or smoking. I know that you are the most wonderful and loving mother and if I could have voted I would have chosen you as the best mother in the world.' She sealed those wonderful words with a kiss. This lifted my spirit and made my body tremble even though I knew that this was the mother that would leave me one day soon.

After two months I returned to work feeling miserable and empty, especially whenever I looked out of my office window to see if my mother would pass. This brought tears to my eyes. I also dreaded that maybe something else was going to happen.

With all this happening in Zimbabwe, my fiancé decided to go ahead of me to Australia and get his family to prepare everything before I arrived with my children so that life would be easier for us. His plan was that we would just fly down and walk straight into a new home. All the preparations for the wedding would have been made before I arrived. In the meantime, he would be working and also sorting out our immigration papers.

So, once again, I was at home alone with my children. We were all so excited about the new baby Rosie, that nobody missed Dave too much; we all just carried on with life normally, knowing that one day my boyfriend would send for us all. Every month he would send flowers and money to help and I felt that at least there was someone out there who really cared about us. As I looked at my children, for the first time I realised they were all so very different looking. I joked to myself that all that was left was Chinese. Nevertheless, I was the proud mother of these wonderful assorted children. I see myself as a very playful mother but very strict and loving. We had such a bond that we just couldn't live separately.

When my children Shane and Aida were growing up they were very supportive children who knew how to love their family so much. Shane always did things in the house to help with all the chores and would also help with Aida when she got sick from time to time. She would get huge lumps behind her ears, a high temperature and suffered so much pain that I would have to take her to the doctor. He always prescribed antibiotics but never explained why she suffered from these lumps—he didn't know. Shane was just a blessing in my life—someone to hold on to. Without him I don't think I would have been strong enough to keep going. I had no husband at that time. We planned our lives together, making Sunday a special day of thanks to the Lord. We called this our 'family day', when we would enjoy ourselves, have the best meal we could and just simply love and help each other with ideas. My son was so clever at school and one of the best athletes too—bringing home trophies and certificates of all sorts, just as his parents had before him. I was so proud of him all of his school life and never missed one of my beloved, handsome, Muslim-looking son's games.

My little girl, Aida, was also very clever at school, despite missing out on a lot of schooling because of her illness. She would always take top of the class but at sports she usually came last. She was just not as strong as the other children. Aida was very similar to me in many ways; we looked like twins and also had the same personality ways—it was just that one looked older than the other. We both kept our hair very long, just the way we both liked it. She was always keen to help around the house and at the age of five she started wearing aprons and to learn to cook. By the age of nine she knew how to bake and would make some delicious meals for our Sunday 'family day'. She would always wear polka dotted aprons—green with white dots—that she sewed herself. After she had made a meal the kitchen would be spotless with no sign of any mess from all the baking and cooking that had gone on—just a proud little girl ready to share the fruits of her labour with all her family. Of course, my heart would be bursting with joy and pride at this point and this is how I felt with each and every day of my life with Aida.

Every Sunday Aida would dress in her best clothes and wait, together with her brother, for the church bus to pick them up. This was not something I had to persuade her to do—she just enjoyed going to church. She would tell me, 'Mommy, I have to go to church so that God can look after my family because that is all I have left.' After church, we would sometimes continue our family day by going to the local park, which was like heaven to us. I could sit for hours just watching my children playing and admiring the flowers around us including the rose bushes, which were always in flower and I would always think how lucky I was. After a while I would be running around with the children—not like a mother but just like a child. As we left the park, the children would make sure that they had pinched a few flowers for their precious mother. Even when the other children were born, we never forgot our 'family day' or any of the other things we enjoyed—like having a family bath together and we never ran out of bubble bath in spite of us not having much money. Eventually, of course, the bath got too small for us all to bathe together and as Shane got older he grew shy of bathing with the girls. We were such a close family at this time—my children never once failed to kiss me good morning or goodnight.

I managed to buy a small sewing machine and always sewed my girls—Aida, Jane and Rosie—the same clothes just to show them that we belong together. Our home was a wonderful place to be—just like heaven to us. We were poor but we loved everything we had. In the kitchen, the cupboards where we kept the pots didn't even have any doors. I don't know why, but this is where our chickens always came to lay their eggs so we used to have nesting mother chickens in our kitchen pots. This was OK but the chickens gave me problems. There was a Muslim mosque near our house and when they held their service on Fridays, my chickens would run in, shit and mingle with the congregation when they were trying to pray. The priest was not at all happy with this but eventually we became very best friends and I did a lot of work for the mosque. On the kitchen counter I kept all sorts of birds—apart from the chickens. One bird we truly loved was called 'Danny Boy', a cockatiel who used to sing to us every morning. All our birds had names and there was nothing we didn't love and look after. In my garden I always planted rose trees and also marigold flowers, which were my favourite.

When I was working for the Ministry of Health in Gweru, we had a lot of different expatriate doctors from other countries who were employed by the Government, as there was, at that time, a shortage of qualified doctors in Zimbabwe. I made good friends with one of the doctors called Elizabeth ('Liz') Mason who worked dealing with little children. She was a young, white lady form Britain who had just qualified as a doctor and I found her to be a wonderful person who would go out of her way just to please and to help everybody that she possibly could. Many times she would even work extra hours without getting paid. She was such a beautiful person that even the Provincial Medical Director (Doctor Shiva), who was a Muslim, fell head over heels in love with her and they eventually got married and later started a family. Working with Doctor Mason and Doctor Shiva, we all developed a close bond and I had so much respect for these two people. I hoped they felt the same way about me. One day, Doctor Shiva called me into his office and asked me to sit down. This sounded so formal that I was shocked and worried that maybe I was going to be fired or something serious. I sat there waiting nervously but what he wanted to say was that he had made out a cheque for five hundred dollars for myself and my children—Shane, Aida, Jane and Rosie—and that I should use it to take them on a nice holiday somewhere. Of course, I broke down in tears and thanked him over and over again and then searched out Liz to thank her too. At that time Liz used to come in and out of my home quite frequently, just to check on my children's health. In my heart I thought that these two were also angels sent to me by God. This would be my very first holiday with my precious children. I couldn't believe that all this was true. I knew I would have a really great time just loving each of them and it came at just the right time, having just lost my wonderful mother—everybody at work used to call my mother 'Lady Jane'.

We started planning our holiday straight away and decided to go to Gabarone, the capital of Botswana, a country to the south-west of Zimbabwe. We booked our hotel for one week and after we all arrived by train, we had something to eat before deciding to have an early night. We intended to get up nice and fresh, ready to explore in the morning and to enjoy this new town.

The next few days it was just as if I was in wonderland—playing with my children in the park, swimming with them, eating junk food and wandering around the most fascinating shops. There was nothing like this in our country. At night I played in the shower with all my children before dinner. After that, we would all have a meal in the hotel. The whole family was so nicely done up, the children's faces clean and shining after their shower. It looked and felt so beautiful in my mind that I felt overwhelmed that I had been given the chance to enjoy myself with my children for the very first time.

When our week was over I cried all the way back to Zimbabwe because of the sheer joy of having had such a nice time with my children for the first time. I was also grateful to have such a good friend. She was going to be a treasure for life and I felt as though my heart was about to explode with all the love just for our little circle of happiness.

9

Australian Interlude

Our baby, Rosie, was two years old when my boyfriend sent for just her and myself to join him in Australia. He said that he wanted us to marry first, while sorting things out with the immigration people, then we could send for the other children later. I was so excited and looking forward to being reunited with Dave that maybe I failed to see how this was affecting my other children. My little girl, Sunshine, was especially troubled by my going. She was so attached to me that sometimes I really thought we were inseparable. Often if one of us left, the other would get ill and that is why I had never allowed my children to go anywhere without me. I had been parted from them when I was on holiday in Malawi but then just thinking about my children left behind made me feel ill and so sometimes I had to pretend to be having a nice time. When we flew back home after the holiday, I had missed my children so much that just seeing them, especially Sunshine, made me fall to my knees, crying with joy. When my mother was alive she had them to stay for only two weeks but I missed them so much that I hired a taxi to go and collect them before their holiday was up. Even then I cried with joy to see my babies. This kind of love is beautiful, of course, but it also has a lot of damaging consequences. For instance, it makes you possessive and scared of letting them go and it's painful to share your children with anyone else—you just want to keep all your babies next to you and smother them like a mother hen.

By this time my son was older and doing a lot of sport, winning trophies like I had done at his age, and doing well at school. My daughter Sunshine was just twelve and also doing well at school. Aida's best school friend's mother was the manageress of Truworth's store—a leading fashion retailer in Gweru—and she saw the potential in Aida to become a model. Aida subsequently modelled clothes for Truworth's and also Edgar's—a fashion chain store. Nippy was four by this time and turning into an adorable and accomplished little girl. From about the age of three she liked music so much that she danced and sang whenever the radio was playing. I entered her into talent shows and she would always take first or second place against much older children. She would wear very short mini dresses and dance to songs by Michael Jackson, who was her favourite singer. Aida used to stand in the wings of the stage and prompt her in the dance moves. The only time that Aida wasn't there to help her was when she got sick and was rushed to hospital. The show had already started and when Nippy looked to the wings for moves from Aida she was not there to show her. Nippy was only able to come fifth in that show. She never called me Mommy because she always thought Aida was her mother and I was called by my first name from when she could speak.

Jane and Rosie

We went into a whirl of preparation for our departure. I put in my notice at work and made arrangements with my auntie Elena and a friend who worked with me to look after my children for a short time while I would be in Australia preparing everything ready for them to join us.

Aida (centre) modelling for Truworth's store

The following month I left for Australia with Rosie, catching the largest plane I had ever seen. I flew with the Australian airline Qantas (Queensland and Northern Territory Aerial Services) from Harare to Perth. The treatment on the plane by the airhostesses was great, with an excellent supper and a nice film after to help to relax me. The only problem, of course, was a deep feeling of unhappiness and sadness that I had left behind my other children. That night I don't even remember sleeping. This was my first time on a plane going so far without all my children. I prayed silently all the way, especially for my little 'Sunshine' whom I was already missing.

We arrived on 1st July 1985, early in the morning, with the sun already shining brightly. The sunshine made me optimistic for the future and as I walked from the plane with my little Rosie towards a new life, I thought it would be the best day I had had for a long time. I walked through the unfamiliar surroundings and the crowds of people and there, right in front of me, I saw my fiancé, Dave. I can remember running to him breathlessly and we started kissing. Nothing could separate our lips—it was like they were stuck together. We forgot all about Rosie and just clung together. Even when we caught the bus our lips were sealed together the whole way but we lovingly held our baby who was so shocked, wondering what was going on. We reached the flat that Dave had got ready for us and later we made sure we blessed every room by kissing and making love in each of the rooms. The sweet feelings we had right then mixed with the pain that stabbed our hearts for all the lost moments. Tears fell down our cheeks as we surrendered to that wonderful feeling that lights up your whole body and gives you such a glow of happiness.

Aida and Rosie

I used to phone my children twice a week to make sure they were all alright. I would always tell them we were going to send for them as soon as we had settled a few of the problems. After a while we set our wedding day, which was going to be in about two months time, and then we set about making all the necessary arrangements. I also met my in-laws, Rosalind and Jack, who seemed to like me.

Our small flat became like heaven to us, although we didn't have much furniture. I kept our home clean and tidy and after my fiancé left for work at the local school each morning, I would take Rosie and go shopping at the little centre not far from where we lived. This was also such a wonderful experience, looking at all the nice things in the shops. It was difficult to know what to buy because everything was so beautiful—something you could only dream about.

Playing with Rosie in the park

At weekends, when my fiancé didn't have to work at the school, we would go to the huge park just around the corner from our house. This had a very big dam and a nice playground for Rosie and here we would hire some bicycles and put our child in the little carrier on the back. Then we would cycle around the dam with plenty of enthusiasm and lots and lots of laughter. Some weekends we used to go to the zoo. This made me so excited—just like being a little girl again, remembering all the animals that we had had on our farm when I had been growing up. These animals, of course, were very different from the animals I had known and this made it all the more exciting for us because everything was so new to me. On some occasions we would go into town just to look around at furniture for our new home that we would get when we got married. We wanted to make our first proper home together the most beautiful home in the world. We did everything together to try to make our dreams come true.

One time, after being in Perth for about a month, I decided to visit my Auntie Miriam, who lived on the outskirts of Perth. This journey took almost three hours by train. My journey out there was fine, but the return journey was not so good. I was not used to travelling on trains and, as I sat there watching the countryside race past in a blur, it sped along so fast, giving me no time to think. I suddenly found myself arriving in a little town that was strange to me. I had got lost. I had no choice but to telephone Dave—in tears—to come and get me. I cried and cried while I waited on the busy station, as I was simply terrified of the trains by this time.

Despite my occasional panics with unfamiliar things, we had an almost perfect life. The one problem that we did have was my very nosy mother-in-law-to-be. She always wanted to know everything and always seemed to be around our flat doing something or other and she gave us no space to ourselves. One day, Dave said he wanted to take us on a two-week holiday to Adelaide. This was going to be a very long journey by car and it made me very excited. What I did not know was that my mother-in-law, who had decided on something very different, would change the plans. She decreed that she and her husband would be accompanying us on our trip. On this little holiday we had to travel for several hours and we eventually arrived at the little hotel, where she had booked just one room for all of us to share. I was appalled to see that there was only a curtain dividing the room. There was an old, springy bed that made a dreadful, squeaky noise with even the smallest movement. That night we all went to watch a concert in a very big hall. Later on we went to a dance where we all had a few drinks and Dave and I danced through the night. Dave's mother had decided to ignore me all night and she acted like I did not exist. This made me feel awful and I had all sorts of thoughts running through my head. I made up my mind to try to ignore this treatment while we were out and to fix my mother-in-law when we got back to the hotel by having Dave shower with me. We played like children. We even went as far as playing on the old spring bed, making such a noise. The next morning you could have cut the atmosphere with a knife. She looked at me icily and after breakfast she took out her camera. She took plenty of photos but she always made sure that I was not in the shot. This quiet feud continued for the entire holiday and I was at a loss as to understanding any of it. In contrast to his wife's behaviour, Dave's father was just so wonderful and kind to me and to our daughter. Rosie was his first grandchild and you could see that he really cared for her.

In the following days I did my best to enjoy the break and we went to the coast several times, watching the huge ships in the harbour. I remember that we also saw at that time a huge whale. This was the first time I had seen such a thing. It seemed to be looking straight at me with its piercing black eyes and I ran away, frightened. As soon as we got back to our house in Perth, I immediately ran to phone my children back home in Africa.

Aida in school uniform

One morning, I don't know why, I was feeling miserable and missing my children even more than usual. I had a strange feeling that something was wrong with Sunshine or maybe one of the other children. I had to phone Africa straight away and when I got through the first voice I heard was that of my little Sunshine, who said 'Mommy, please come home. If you don't I am going to get sick and die.' These words sent a chill right through me. They were devastating words for a mother to hear from one of her children, so far away. It was so frightening for me to hear these harsh words and, through my tears, I promised her that I would see what could be done to change things and told her I would phone her at the end of the week. That week passed so slowly with me feeling so miserable and sad, my daughter's words going round and round in my head. I phoned again at the end of the week and Sunshine repeated those same, awful words—'Mommy, please come home. If you don't I am going to get sick and die.' Over the next month I worried and worried and became terribly afraid for the safety of my children back in Africa. I longed to be with them and this caused problems between Dave and me. We argued constantly and fought over silly things. I told him what my daughter had said but he only responded that she was very spoilt and that she just wanted me all to herself. I cried and cried during this month and finally he gave in and paid for a ticket back to Africa for me.

The next few days leading up to my departure were very difficult to get through. They were one big nightmare, as I was being torn between my fiancé and the children I dearly loved. It seemed that I just didn't know how to be happy anymore. I hardly spoke or laughed and this was unfair on little Rosie. She simply wanted her old mother back. We took a bus ride into town to take Rosie shopping but we had such a miserable time that we returned with only a pint of bottled milk. Even on the bus we were fighting and quarrelling about my returning home. Dave said I had wasted his money on air tickets without doing anything of importance that could have helped us with immigration and getting my family into the country. When I thought I just couldn't take any more of his criticism, I grabbed my child and jumped out of the bus just before it stopped. I landed on my hands and knees, but luckily neither of us was hurt. My boyfriend simply carried on with his journey, leaving us to sort ourselves out. I had no idea where I was, but started to walk and walk for hours until I stopped to find out when the next bus was due. This is truly what they call stubbornness. Eventually we made it home and as we walked through the door late that night, Dave took Rosie gently from my arms, put her down and took me by the hand. He led me into the shower where we turned on the water—still fully clothed—and held onto one another, crying. Showering together was one of our everyday things.

Dave and I lay awake side by side all night before my flight back to Africa—sleeping was impossible. We just lay there talking until the sun shone in through the windows. We felt we needed to talk all night just to fit in everything we needed to say to each other and because this is all we had to last us until we met again. He took me, with his child, by taxi to the airport and we both cried all the way there. As we walked slowly through the airport, we would stop every now and again and hold each other and then start crying all over again. This made it impossible to keep up and we were running late for the flight. We stopped again at the departure gate and he held me and his daughter tightly to him. We all stood there crying like children and I felt a stabbing pain that made me feel so weak that I was in danger of dropping our child. As I looked up into Dave's beautiful blue eyes I felt sure my heart would stop beating and I would fall down dead. I was terrified that this was the end and I would never see him again. His whole shirt was wet with our tears. Rosie was crying too as I walked slowly towards the plane with her. As I looked back and saw him standing there I panicked. I broke into a run then because I knew if I didn't get away quickly I wouldn't go through with it. If I wasn't quick I would just run straight back into his loving arms. I boarded the plane, hugging my daughter to me and choking on my tears.

Despite my sorrow, I knew, as I sat on the plane making its way back to Zimbabwe, that I had made the right decision. My children were more important to me than anything in the world—including the man I loved.

10

A mother's nightmare

The day before I left Australia I had made arrangements with the friend who had been helping to care for my children to drive down from Gweru and meet me at the airport. I knew that I would be feeling dreadful and would need help with Rosie. I didn't feel that in my distressed state I would be the best person to be responsible for a small child. I would need the attention of someone who was sensible and sober in mind to take over. I had met this friend at the local church in Gweru where we attended mass together. She was a church missionary from England and her name was Denise Vandenwalt. She had come to Zimbabwe with her young son aged eleven to try and help people by spreading the word of God with the Bible and also singing the most wonderful hymns. Over the years Denise and I became very close friends. We looked after each other when help was needed in and out of the home.

When the plane touched down in Harare I hugged Rosie to me and got my things together as fast as possible, making sure I didn't leave a thing on board. I ran through the crowds of people with so much energy that I didn't know where it was coming from. I also noticed that the people on the other side of the barrier were looking at me and feeling sorry because they could all see how swollen my eyes were. The crying didn't stop—with each and every breath I just cried more and more. When I saw Denise standing at the far end of the arrivals lounge I almost jumped with joy and relief that at least there was someone to take me to my children as fast as possible. I hadn't told her why I was returning home so soon and what my little Aida had said to me previously; all I told her is that I was missing my children so much that I had returned. This was very true, of course, and her knowing the type of mother I was she found this plausible.

I was able to relax a little when we got into the car with Rosie and my entire luggage loaded. As we drove along we exchanged details of all the different things that had been happening over the past weeks. Sitting there and just listening to her talk and later singing on the journey back home just put back into me all the little happy memories of our wonderful friendship. This is when I did stop crying. I lay back and just enjoyed looking at all the wonderful buildings and trees as we passed, thinking in my heart that this is so beautiful and our God had given us this chance to enjoy the world and be happy. We finally got home and, kissing my friend goodbye and thanking her for everything, I ran like lightening to knock on my front door. With my heart beating fast and hard, with big, blazing eyes and with a smile that was so big it almost tore my lips, I stood waiting for the door to open.

Meeting and holding my children then was the best experience I ever felt in my life. If I could only have carried all of them, putting them into my body just to keep them safe, I would have done it. I kissed them all over and over again. We jumped straight into the bed all together, talking, asking lots of questions and enjoying some of the nice goodies I had bought on the plane and in Australia. The love for my children was so strong that it gave me no time to think of the love I had left in Australia with a broken heart. I knew that the decision I had made was the one I wanted and needed and I had to carry it through no matter what.

During the first few days of being home with my children, I could see there was nothing wrong with Aida so I was happy that all was OK. The only problem for me was that I was beginning to miss my Dave in Australia. I missed him so much that sleeping was impossible at times and I would just lie half awake, wondering why he wasn't contacting me anymore; had he found someone else or had he lost complete interest in me? I thought maybe I was giving him so many problems that he couldn't cope anymore or that his mother had advised him to give me up. All of these negative thoughts were running through my head and there was just no space for positive thinking. As on previous stressful occasions, this resulted in my suffering from migraine headaches.

My landlady had given me back my little flat, so I worked hard to get that sorted out to make a nice home for us all again. As soon as I could I applied for my old job back and I was so lucky—they accepted me back straight away. I spent one full week with the children, then went back to work the following week. This was all part of my effort to keep busy until my fiancé sent for me again as he had promised.

The morning I started back at work I felt like an outcast and also very silly and stupid because I was back where I had started. I thought that now people won't think very much of me and maybe people were also thinking my man had finished with me. All the negative feelings that had plagued me before came flooding back, and my self-esteem was very low. With prayer, I soon fell into my old regular pattern of coping with life and decided that my children were much more important than people talking and just pushed my pride aside. I did my best with a positive attitude and with understanding and kindness to just about everyone, because at this stage I was very vulnerable to anything.

Shortly after my return to Zimbabwe, my father gave me my mother's deep freeze and asked me to use it in remembrance of her using it in the proper way—letting nobody touch or play near the fridge. Of course, keeping a large, deep fridge with nothing in it was pointless, so I came up with a little business idea. I decided to buy live chickens, then clean and slaughter them before putting them in the freezer. I would sell them to my work friends and some of our neighbours. This would all be run from our small flat. I bought a delivery bicycle that could carry forty live chickens—twenty in the front and twenty in the back, in boxes from the nearest farm. I would do this every other day, starting the minute I got home from work. By the time the chickens had been killed, cleaned, dressed, packed and put in my mother's deep freeze ready for selling the next morning, it would be 2 a.m. This was hard work for a woman but that is exactly what I did in my spare time. My son was now fifteen years of age and he helped me with a lot of the work and also with my business planning and decision-making. We would sit together as a family as we worked and we talked about buying a house with a swimming pool. A lot of the white people were leaving Zimbabwe because of the worsening situation and their houses were going at very cheap prices but at the same time the prices for renting flats in town were going up so we could see our chance might come. Every bit of money we made we saved for our new dream home.

After I'd been back at work for about three months, my daughter, Aida, decided she would only bathe when I got back home in the evening so when I finished work—at about five o'clock—I headed straight home and we all (apart from my son, of course, as he was getting big now and could not bathe with us girls) jumped into our bubble bath. As we sat down in the water, I noticed that Sunshine's stomach was bulging just a little. I asked her why she hadn't told me her stomach was swollen and she just said 'mommy remember you told me when a young girl is about to have her periods her tummy blows up'. She sat there in the soapy water looking so young and vulnerable. As I looked back at her I felt so scared because I knew instantly that my little girl was sick. Something was terribly wrong.

I jumped out of the water knowing that what I had dreaded throughout Sunshine's life had happened. I had always felt that something terrible was going to happen to my daughter and now I felt that fear was going to strangle me to death.

I could hardly breathe. I told her to jump out of the bath and to get dressed as fast as she possibly could. I don't know how I dressed myself because in seconds I was ready to go and we were leaving the house. We could not afford a taxi and the buses did not always run along the road where we lived. Gweru hospital was quite a distance away and we could not walk so the only option for us was to stand by the side of the road and hitch a lift from a passer-by. Being so desperate I was prepared to jump into anybody's car, without any fear for our safety, just to get my precious Aida to the hospital. We stood there for more than an hour until someone stopped at long last. It was a man from the Zimbabwean SPCA in his little van to pick up stray dogs. When the man noticed the state I was in and learned where we were going he did not charge us anything at all for the lift. All the way there I felt just like one of those stray dogs that were barking and yapping behind us in the back of his little van. Through the glass I could see the dogs' frightened, piercing eyes. They must have been wondering what was going to happen to them, just like me. On arrival at the hospital he dropped us right at the entrance and still had not asked us any questions. I was so grateful for his politeness and kindness.

Shane, Aida and me looking concerned by Aida's condition

Our ordeal was far from over, as we were then kept waiting at the hospital outpatients' department for almost three hours. I was feeling tired by this time and became more anxious than ever before. When our turn came, the doctor walked in and when he examined Aida he took his time and was very gentle with her. He set your heart at ease with his manner, but when he finally gave us his diagnosis it came as such a big shock for us both that we just broke down in tears. I held my Aida in my arms as the doctor told me, after taking a long, deep breath, that she had to be admitted into hospital. He thought she had a kidney infection on the right side and needed urgent medical attention plus some tests that had to be done the very next day. This was why she had been accumulating fluids in her stomach and body. He reassured me that this was something very common and could easily be treated with medication, that I mustn't worry—my daughter was going to be alright. I still felt a deep, intense fear for my daughter and instinctively knew this was not true. Somehow I think that if you truly love your child you always have a motherly instinct that tells you. I don't know how, but you can feel when something is seriously wrong. Both Aida and I just clung together because she did not want to stay in the hospital and she was also telling me 'You see, Mommy, I told you I was going to get sick'.

When the nurse came to collect Aida to take her to her bed for the night I was allowed to accompany her. We walked hand in hand along the corridor into a small dark room with two beds. The room felt as if there were no air inside and most of the linen on the bed looked old and soiled, with not a proper hygienic smell when I pulled back the sheets. In the bed next to Aida was an old lady who was weeping quietly. She had sores all over her body and looked a frightful sight, with that indefinable kind of smell that made you feel like vomiting. Just looking at all this made me so sick that I had to run into the dirty toilets vomiting. I had to make an enormous effort to control myself because of my frightened little girl. When Aida was asleep and safe, the little old lady had started crying once again so I asked her if she was OK and whether I could do anything to help. Standing there next to her, I could see that this lady was in no position to use her hands to eat or even have a drink of water. My heart just ached to help her. I automatically peeled one of her bananas, which were rotting on the bedside table but which were still just fit to eat. There didn't seem to be anything else around. She just gobbled up the banana so fast that within seconds she was finished. It was like she was starving. I then raised her head and put a pillow behind it, put a napkin on her chest and gave her some fresh water to drink. It was obvious from the way she drank it that the nurses were not looking after this poor little lady. I resolved there and then that as long as I was going to be around I would always bring food and drink and look after her while Aida was in hospital. I wanted to try to make her well again and I was sure I could do it just by giving her some affection as her sister in Christ. The thing that pleased me the most is when this lady looked at me, gratitude was written in her eyes. I just smiled. Looking back at her as I was leaving I noticed that although her face was full of pain, she tried to smile at me.

That evening was just the beginning of the one hundred kisses that I promised to give Aida each and every morning and evening. Each one was like a knife going through my heart. My love for her was much, much more than any love that could ever be explained. Leaving the hospital without Aida just made me feel sick inside. I just walked all the way back home in some sort of daze, without looking for transport or even feeling the distance or the weather or whether it was night or day. But I reached home eventually.

I explained to my children about Sunshine having to have some tests done at the hospital and also that her kidneys had an infection. I reassured them that the doctors would soon treat it—there was nothing to worry about. We had a simple meal and all the while I was trying hard not to show any distress or worry about Aida. Before we all jumped into bed, my two daughters sleeping with me, and my son safe in the next room, I decided to get us all together for prayers. We held hands and prayed for Aida and the rest of our family. I kissed everybody goodnight and counted my blessings as they all went to sleep. I just couldn't sleep though and stayed awake through the dark hours looking at Aida's pillow and feeling a dreadful emptiness. As I lay there, I promised myself never, ever to leave my children again for any period of time, but I think I was really looking to blame myself for what had happened. Having left my children and gone off to Australia I felt I had let them all down. Maybe Aida would not have had this infection. I was all alone in that big flat with nobody to comfort me. I knew that I must protect my children and I would never make them feel any fear so I put on a brave face for them. I just had to pray to make me stronger than what I was feeling.

I knew that I wouldn't be able to go back to work in the near future so I informed my boss. I explained about my little girl and he was very understanding. He told me I could come back when everything was OK and he promised to try to help with the payment of my salary and whatever I needed.

Looking back now I think that maybe my beautiful Sunshine knew that something terrible was going to happen in her young life. My little Aida's favourite song was 'Shining Star' (I cannot remember the artist). She always said that she was the brightest star in the sky and if we were ever to miss her we only had to look up at the night sky and we would see her because 'I will be the shiniest star, looking down and protecting my family'. She just knew.

Shane, Aida, Jane and Rosie

11

The nightmare continues

The next morning I woke up early with Aida on my mind. I hurriedly got everyone ready for nursery and school so that I could get an early start at the hospital and made sure that I had clean clothing for my daughter and something nice for her to eat. I also took food for the little old lady in the next bed, as she was, in my heart, part of my responsibility. I couldn't bear the fact that nobody at the hospital looked like they cared about her.

I arrived at the hospital to find that my daughter was in a cheerful mood, laughing as she always did, and with such a bright, happy spirit that anyone who was to meet her would know instantly that she was a child of God. Everyone would always just fall in love with her straight away. Her happy mood made me feel better about the whole situation. I told her all about what her brother and sisters had been doing and then I set about tidying her up ready for the doctor's visit. I put some fruits in a bowl by Aida's bed and then turned to do the same for the lady in the next bed. I stopped in astonishment as I realised that Aida had already started looking after her. Just imagine, a girl of only thirteen years of age actually thinking of helping someone in that condition! I would have thought that a girl would be frightened by the situation, but not Aida. I choked back my tears and thought to myself, 'Well, that's my daughter.'

The doctor also seemed to be in a more cheerful mood as he strode into Aida's room. It made me more confident and I started to believe that there really was nothing to worry about. The doctor examined my daughter and wrote out a prescription for some very expensive drugs, saying that I must immediately go the pharmacy in the town and get the drugs for her.

I left the hospital straight away and managed to get a lift straight to the pharmacy. I gave the pharmacist the prescription and he asked how old the patient was. When I told him that my daughter was only thirteen years old, the man became very flustered and his face turned bright red. 'This girl is too young to have this medication. If she has it, it will be very dangerous for her—she is just too young.' Nevertheless, he gave me the drug and I raced back to the hospital with it, feeling puzzled and frightened. I resolved that I would speak to the doctor again before the drug was administered, as surely he would know much more about his patient and the treatment she should be having.

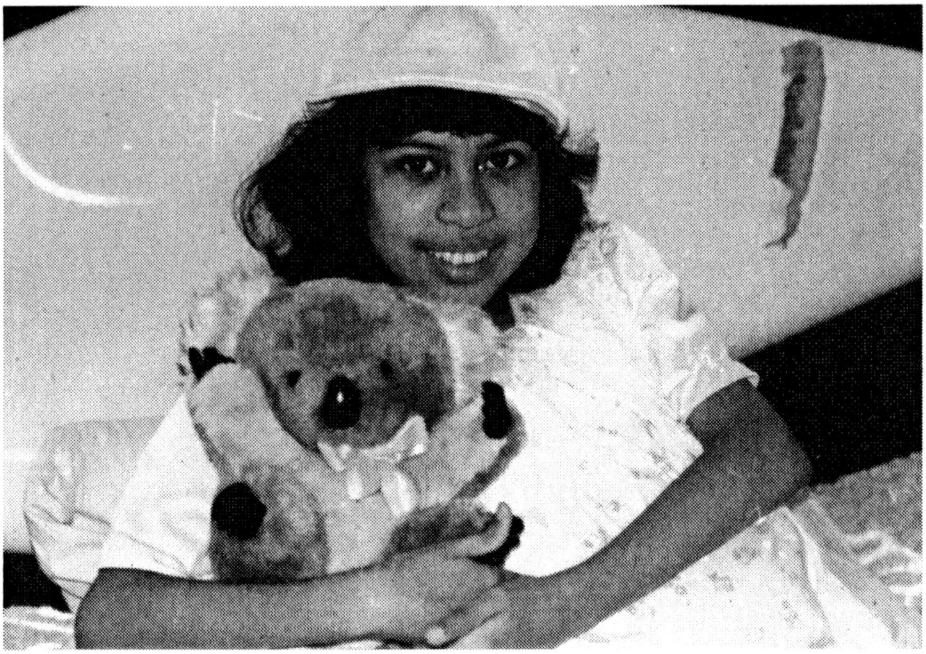

Aida and friend

Back on the ward I refused to let the nurses give the medicine to Aida and insisted that they call the doctor so that I could speak to him about what the pharmacist had said. Within minutes the doctor was at my side and I repeated the conversation I'd had at the pharmacy. He immediately became very angry and shouted at me, 'Who is the doctor here? Or do you want to become a doctor now?' He warned me that if my daughter was going to get well then she had to have this medication to get rid of the infection without delay. Once again, I felt confused but now I had to put my trust in this man who really looked like he knew what he was doing. The doctor administered the medication himself with some water and then left Aida's bedside without another word. He was obviously not pleased with me.

Aida's school friends had rung me to find out how she was and had arranged to come to see her at the hospital. Aida was so excited that we had hardly thought of the doctor at all. An hour later, just before her friends were due to arrive to visit, Aida started a bout of severe diarrhoea. It was non-stop—the white sheets were a complete mess, the room smelled awful and her friends were on their way. I tried desperately to get her cleaned up. The nurses didn't help. They just silently handed me some clean sheets and left me to get on with it. As I worked, I realised that my child was going to be very sick indeed. I worked frantically to sort out the bed and her nightclothes but her friends arrived before I'd finished and she was so embarrassed that she burst into tears. I had to tell her friends to leave as Aida wasn't very well. They were disappointed but left immediately. I was left with my precious baby and I took her in my arms behind the closed curtains around the bed and hugged her and comforted her until she had calmed down. Aida never wanted her friends to visit again.

Less than an hour later she was in a mess again as the diarrhoea hit her once more. Although the doctor had been informed the first time the diarrhoea struck her, he still hadn't come to see Aida. I knew we shouldn't delay so I ran to fetch him, begging him to please, please come to see my child. I raced back to her bedside and cleaned her up again, silently praying that she wouldn't get alarmed about anything. The doctor arrived and calmly informed us that there was nothing to worry about as her stomach was just cleaning itself out. As soon as the doctor had left, the same thing happened again but this time it was even more frightening as her face started to turn bright red and swell up. She looked desperately ill so I ran again to fetch the doctor but, as he'd gone off duty, I had to find another one. He came straight away and examined Aida. He instructed me to get her as fast as possible to Parirenyatwa Hospital in Harare where they had better facilities. At this point my beautiful daughter started to have what looked like a fit and she then went straight into some sort of coma. I screamed for the nurses and, with the doctor barking out instructions, they set up a drip. I looked at my baby lying there with a swollen face and her eyes now closed and I started shaking. This was much worse than I had feared and I prayed for God to wait and not take my daughter. I ran as fast as my legs would go to the call box. When I got there I could hardly speak, the words wouldn't come out—I thought they were choking me—and so a stranger came forward, took the phone from my hands and helped me to make the arrangements for an ambulance to Harare. He had to do most of the talking, as I just couldn't make any sense in my panic.

It seemed an age before our ambulance arrived, complete with a nurse to accompany us on our four hundred mile journey. I got into the back with Aida and sat holding her drip while she lay next to me. It puzzled me that the nurse sat in the front with the driver and I felt they were both ignoring us. After driving along for about two hours, we suddenly stopped and the driver and the nurse started what seemed to me like a picnic. I, of course, was still holding the drip at this time. There was nowhere to put the bag of fluid and I just had to hold it up high so that it could run properly. I don't know why the nurse didn't do this. Every time I looked at my poor child, lying there, suffering, my grief and fear got deeper and deeper. Something in me just snapped and I started screaming at them to please carry on because my child was going to die if we delayed. I threatened to report them to the Ministry of Health and to tell the Ministry that they had been eating while my baby was dying. With this they suddenly got very scared and we set off again—still with the nurse in the front seat with the driver and I was left, yet again, to care for my daughter in the back of the ambulance. There didn't seem to be anything else that I could do apart from to keep praying. There was not one second of that journey that went by that I didn't pray—and cry.

It was late by the time we arrived at the hospital in Harare and things changed straight away. There were people to meet us and I noticed as we entered the hospital that it smelled fresh at least. We were shown to a nice, clean room and you could really feel the different environment—this felt like a proper hospital. Aida was seen immediately by a specialist—someone who knew about and dealt with people with kidney infections. For the next few days she made good progress, slowly regaining consciousness and beginning to laugh again. She made many friends in the ward around her including the doctor who was treating her. He now also called my daughter by her nickname 'Sunshine' and told me that she brightened his spirits.

As Aida improved I began to worry more about the children I had left behind at home. I had left them in the care of a very good friend from work, called Sipwe, who I knew would care for my children as if they were her own. I had also arranged for my Auntie Elena to help her with the cooking and cleaning and looking after Rosie who was now going on three. I worried about Rosie in particular as she was so young and would miss me and I knew I would have to go and collect her as soon as I possibly could.

After some tests, the doctor told me that Aida's right kidney was completely damaged and that the left one was also now infected. She was put on tablets to help her pass water and several other tablets but these seemed to make her condition worse, not better.

Me, Shane, Jane and Rosie

Aida had lost a lot of weight but seemed to keep herself cheerful. In April 1987 she was put on to a dialysis machine to purify her blood and to do this the doctor had to place a shunt each time into one of her little veins. Now, this is not a serious operation but it was nerve-wracking and it hurt me—I could feel physical pain—every time he did it. Sometimes the shunt would not work properly and the doctor would have to look for another vein on a different hand or leg. Of course, the blood should have been the same blood group as her own but one day the nurses gave her the wrong blood. As I sat by her side, I saw my daughter's face just swell up before my eyes and she changed colour as I watched. I immediately started screaming for the nurses and by the time the nurses got the doctor, she was turning purple. The doctor straight away realised what had happened and switched off the machine. He gave her some sort of medication and she slept for the rest of the day. The next day she got up early and I tried to feed her but her appetite was going and she just had a little nibble of food.

To add to Aida's problems, her shunt became blocked so she had to have another operation to insert one in her other hand. On the day this was due to be done, she got up with a painful migraine headache. It was so bad that she screamed in agony and the doctor tried all sorts of medication to help her but when these all failed he told me that he would have to drill some holes in her forehead to relieve the pressure. As he started saying this, Aida began to have a convulsion—something like a fit. This was so frightening and I was to learn later that this was probably an epileptic fit. Her eyes rolled backwards in her head and she was completely out of control. I had never seen anything like this in my life and I felt sure she was dying. I felt devastated. Within seconds the doctor started drilling the holes to release some of the pressure. Later, after she had calmed down, he took X-rays of Aida's head and, as he expected, a blood clot was shown just above her forehead. She would die if this were not removed so a major operation was planned.

The next few days were frantic as they prepared Aida for the operation. They wanted to get her strong enough to withstand it but her legs were swelling because she was passing very little water by now so the nurses prepared to fit a catheter in her bladder. This alarmed Aida and she begged me: 'Please Mommy, please tell them I am still a virgin, mommy, they can't do this to me.' All I could do was hold her and comfort her with whatever strength I could gather. They got the catheter in after a long, hard struggle. Despite the fuss and trauma of this, it did not work very well and when the doctor saw that not much fluid was draining out, he decided to put the shunt in one of her legs. This failed, so he put the shunt in the other leg. This failed too. By this time the doctor was telling me that the only thing left was a kidney transplant. It would need a compatible donor—a family member and the nearest and best hospital for this was in South Africa. In the meantime, my daughter had yet another convulsion and they decided that they had to operate immediately and told me that I must cut off all her beautiful hair. After I'd signed the consent forms for this operation, I set to work on her hair. It was her pride and joy and the thing that she admired most about herself—but it had to go. As I cut it, it felt so alive but I had to keep my crying buried deep inside of me so that she could not see.

As my desperately ill daughter underwent her life-saving operation to remove the blood clot, I sat at the back of the operating room and looked through the open window, pondering why all this pain had been given to one little girl—and one who was truly like an angel. I prayed every second as I waited and asked my Jesus to help us now. Eventually, the doctor came out of the door, saying that Aida was alright and that the blood clot had been successfully removed. Although the operation had left a big, ugly scar across her forehead she soon became my little Sunshine again. This time, though, her weight had dropped drastically. I suspected that when I was not around to feed her, nobody else was looking after her. She once even told me that nobody bothered with her. I tried to be at the hospital as many hours in every day as I could but I had to travel a 25-mile round trip from my Auntie Violet's house where I was staying in Arcadia to the hospital in Harare. I also had to pay my transport costs as well as the hospital fees and try to look after my other children back home in Gweru too. Without God's help I just don't know how I could have done all this.

The blood clot removal had helped Aida and taken her out of immediate danger but she still desperately needed a transplant. My next goal was to get this organised. I asked all my family from both sides to come in for tests to find a compatible donor. It was a bitter let down when not one person came forward from either side apart from me and my son Shane. I was overjoyed when I was found to be the perfect match. To raise the money I had to work fast so when my in-laws came in to see their granddaughter, I threw myself on my knees in front of them and begged my father-in-law to please help me to save my daughter's life. I explained to them that Aida's stomach lining was deteriorating fast because of the kidney problems; she continued to have horribly uncontrollable loose stools and she was accumulating a lot of fluid because of her kidneys not working properly. Without even considering the gravity of my request, they replied that I shouldn't be so silly, that Ighsan's money would arrive soon from Malawi (a pension that was due for the children and me) and that we could use that money when it arrived. I burst into tears. I looked him straight in the eye as the tears ran down my face and without talking out loud, from deep in my heart, said to myself that when he himself was about to die I hoped he would remember my face—the woman who begged him for money to save his grandchild's life.

During the time that she was waiting for her transplant operation, Aida developed huge bedsores. I guess the nurses were not turning her during the night and she was no longer able to turn herself. I could see that the nurses did not even change her sheets or clean her up properly after her bouts of diarrhoea as I sometimes saw that her stools had been allowed to dry against her body. It was so upsetting to see a lovely girl like Aida being treated like this. But worse was to come. The biggest blow of all came when the doctor came to me and said that he was discharging Aida as there was no hope, nothing more they could do, and to take her home. She was dying, he said. I ran to the toilets, vomiting, refusing to listen any more. I took my beloved child home on the most comfortable bus I could find, with lots of pillows to support her. My mind was continually working, trying to think of ways to ask people for help, as I was never going to give up, never!

That journey home was so sad. As I looked around I could see people staring at us, feeling sorry for us, wondering what awful disease she was suffering from. It was impossible not to see that she was desperately ill. She was just a body of bones with skin over them and her legs were now beginning to get stiff, curling up painfully. Her hands were totally stiff too. The only thing that remained of my Sunshine was that beautiful face—just the same little angel who loved the world. As we got near home, Aida whispered to me: 'Mommy, before I die I would like to get married.' In surprise, I asked her 'To whom?' She gave me an even bigger surprise when she answered, 'To you, Mommy. You have been the only person who I have truly loved and I would like you to marry me please Mommy.' I couldn't speak then but at the very next stop—in the small mining town of Kwekwe—I got off and quickly went to a curio shop where I bought the most beautiful ring with a huge orange 'diamond' and a few drinks to celebrate our 'marriage'. When I got back on the bus, I gave the driver one of the drinks and explained to him what was happening. He gave a short speech to those people who were looking on, interested in what we were doing. I could see that he had tears in his eyes and everybody on the bus cheered and wished us well. My little girl was so happy and she gave me one hundred kisses. For the rest of the journey everyone on the bus was completely quiet. All you could hear was the sound of the engine of our bus.

My son, Shane, came with his sisters Jane and Rosie to meet us off the bus when we got back to Gweru. He hadn't seen his sister since she had been in hospital and I will never forget the look on his face when he saw the state his sister was in. I could feel the pain he was feeling and see how he was suffering inside. The whole family was waiting for us back home and we all talked about just about everything. It felt so good to have my little Sunshine back home where she belonged. As I tucked Aida into her bed, I noticed that Shane had redecorated the room. He had also cooked us a nice plate of hot food. I was just so proud—I was speechless. Later that night we all jumped into the one big bed alongside the sick patient and said our prayers. With Aida wedged securely between us, we soon fell asleep.

After a few days at home being cared for, Aida's bedsores began to heal and I began to hope that she was getting well again. There was a peculiar incident one Friday evening when we were all asleep. Aida suddenly stood straight up from the bed in the middle of the night—which she never usually did—and looked fiercely at the end of the room. She had a huge smile on her face and her eyes glowed and sparkled with the reflection of the little light shining from the bathroom. She stretched out her arms and said, 'Grandma Jane, you have come to fetch me.' (She was referring to my mother who had passed away.) My daughter certainly looked as though she was talking to her granny and, for some reason, she had acquired extra strength. She was so strong that I struggled to get her to lie down in the bed and had to shout for help from Shane. Finally she slept again and I quickly, but quietly, removed all the pictures of my mother that had been on the wall. I felt so afraid and curled up next to Aida, smelling her own little fragrance. She had had this unique smell since she was a baby and I loved to snuggle up and smell it on her or on the bedcovers and her pillow. I've never smelled that fragrance on anyone else—it was Aida's alone—and it was so pleasant and calming. I can still smell Aida's fragrance today and feel sure it will be with me forever.

That weekend my father sent a message that I was to go to visit him immediately so I left the children in Shane's charge and hitched a lift to my father's place. He was now staying at the back of some old garages, renting out some rooms but still running his mines. Once I got there he immediately told me of his plans, which involved him selling his plot for seven thousand dollars. He would then give this money to me so that I could use it to help with Aida's kidney transplant. I cried as I took the title deeds from my father's hands and left for home with new hope that I could make this little miracle happen.

Within two days I had found a buyer for the plot with the help of my friend Sipwe. A man who worked for the Gweru town council had the cash available and wanted to buy the plot. He packed the money in a large envelope and we typed out an agreement and exchanged the deeds for the money. I was eager to let my father know the good news straight away so I hitched a lift again to the garage. As I showed him all the money in the envelope, I could see a sad look in his eyes and I knew something was wrong. The next few words he spoke to me broke my heart. I listened in disbelief and sadness as he said to me, 'My daughter, I cannot let you have this money any more because I have decided to keep it and look after your brothers who are all loafers without any jobs and no means of any income.' As I stared back in shock at this I truly felt that I hated this man who called himself my father. It was so painful and the tears were running unchecked down my face. I was amazed at his betrayal—he had promised me that money and he knew what I would have used it for. I just walked away. As I stood at the side of the road waiting to hitch a lift, I promised myself that my next move would be to get my child out of Zimbabwe where they had done nothing for her except damage her life. I was now stronger than ever.

The next day I wasted no time in picking myself up. I got together with a few of my friends to see what ideas we could come up with to raise money to send

Aida to South Africa for the vital transplant. We decided the best way forward was to place a photograph and advertisement on the front page of the *Harare Herald* asking for donations to help pay for her air fare and medical costs.

That night, Aida's condition worsened. Her temperature shot up, she got the migraine headaches more frequently, the fluid was accumulating more, making her stomach very big and she had badly swollen ankles. Seeing my daughter suffering like this made me think I didn't know what to do. But during the night, as I sat by her bedside, I decided to take her back to the hospital from where they had discharged her. By now I was refusing to be refused. We had to go on the bus to the hospital and again I prayed the whole way. I didn't give another thought to the people who had refused to help me—my view was that that was their own sin and they would have to deal with that for themselves—if they did indeed have consciences. When we arrived at the hospital I thought there would we problems but they accepted us back with grace and care.

After a few days, God sent another angel to help me. A man from Britain, who was holidaying in Zimbabwe, had seen my advert in the newspaper and decided that he would like to help us, as his mother had died with the same problem. This gentleman was a Muslim and, to my everlasting regret, I cannot remember his name. I would love to trace this lovely man and thank him once again for his exceptional kindness. My Uncle Ahmed (my mother's sister's husband, who was handling everything for me at this time) made arrangements with this man to meet us at the hospital. Aida and I were so excited. It seemed like we were getting a new lease of life. I made her as comfortable as I possibly could and put a little woolly hat on her head to cover the scar from her operation. She had lots of stitches across her forehead and, of course, her head had been shaved bald. When this tall, dark gentleman arrived he stood at the entrance to the ward and we knew straight away who he was. We both greeted him politely and we knew, just from the way he talked to us, that he was going to sponsor us. Aida thought he was the handsomest man she had ever seen and that he reminded her of a prince.

Later that night, just before I left the hospital, Aida and I shared secrets as I gave her her one hundred kisses goodnight. She whispered in my ear. 'Mommy, I am in love for the first time.' This shocked me and I wondered who she could possibly be in love with. 'Guess, Mommy, guess!' she cried. I couldn't guess so she simply said, 'Our Muslim angel.' Neither of us could remember his name—that's how excited we were. What Aida didn't know was that I too thought of him as an angel sent by God—and a very good-looking one, too. Like they say, 'Like mother, like daughter.' I think we both had a crush on him.

The very next day our Muslim angel had deposited money—thousands of dollars—into my uncle's account to pay for all the costs of the operation plus six seats on the plane for Aida so that she could sleep comfortably during the journey. Of course, that made me so happy and I prayed to God to thank him. During that week the fundraising carried on. The children from my daughter's school, Chaplain High School, Gweru, all donated 20 cents each and the final amount raised there was almost six hundred dollars. We were so grateful for all the people who helped us, giving us what they could afford. The saddest donation came from a 17-year-old Asian girl who was in hospital at the same time as Aida. She had a similar condition to Aida's but her kidney failure was not so serious. She sent us one hundred dollars. When I sent a thank you note just a few days later, I found out that she had died as a result of her condition. I was so shocked by this—it really brought home to me just how sick Aida was. When I had last seen the young Asian girl, she had looked like she would recover quickly—well and strong. She used to visit Aida every day and they became the best of friends. Her passing broke my heart once more and I could not find the words to express my grief so, yet again, I just cried. I never told Aida about her little friend dying.

In the midst of this grief and my worry for Aida, I was unable to keep track of all the monies that were raised for us. I don't know where most of the money went to—I think some of the people were not doing things for the right reasons. I didn't even know exactly how much money our Muslim angel had given us.

The night before we were due to travel to South Africa, I slept peacefully, remembering a story Aida had written in High School about her 'beautiful mother'. This story took first prize and her story about an imaginary trip on a plane took second prize. They were both marked in Cambridge. This memory made me smile as I went to sleep.

The hospital had arranged for an ambulance to take us to the airport with all the travel documents pre-arranged. We were a happy, confident family as we sat on the plane, Aida lying comfortably across the six seats with me on one side of her and her sister Rosie on the other. We had been given another chance by some kind, loving and caring angel that God had sent. On the plane we chatted, with Aida so happy, saying, 'Mommy, you see the essay I wrote about my trip by plane and now I am in an airplane.' The love I felt for her made my heart sing—it was so magical, so real, so beautiful and I had had it from the day I gave birth to Aida.

12

The Nightmare Ends

As our plane landed in South Africa in the late afternoon of 16th June 1987, I was relieved to see an ambulance waiting on the runway to meet us. I just sat a little while until the nurses were there to help Aida. They handled her with so much care as they placed her on the stretcher; then they used a remote device to place the stretcher in the ambulance. I watched with my mouth open—never in my life had I seen such a thing. Although the unfamiliarity of it all frightened me, I gained confidence and renewed hope as I watched the nurses at work and realised that they were smart, professional and competent—they knew exactly what they were doing. I felt even happier as we arrived at the Johannesburg Hospital to be met by my sister Wendy and her husband Brian. At least I would have family here to help me in this strange country. They would be looking after us all.

Aida was admitted to Ward 285 of the Renal Unit and given a lovely big room, with lots of light and fresh air, that was very clean and smelt like a hospital should. We were introduced to the nurses on the ward and the first thing that Aida blurted out was, 'Are you racists?' She had apparently heard there were a lot of race problems in South Africa and she was afraid of being treated badly. She believed everyone must be treated equally. The nurses were obviously very shocked to hear all this from someone so small and ill but I think that it endeared her to them. She bonded with all the nurses who cared for her and they came to truly love her. It was the way she expressed herself—with so much intelligence and dignity—that helped her and this was the first impression people always got when meeting Aida.

That very same day a team of about six specialists came to examine Aida and their verdict was that they had never before seen such a bad case of neglect—especially of a child. They said she had been given many unnecessary tablets, had anaemia and severe malnutrition, diarrhoea, heart failure, an enlarged liver and also severe bedsores that had both fungal and bacterial infections. After a full day of examinations, the doctors called me into a private room and explained to me, in full, their opinion about my daughter. They said that she was a very sick girl and that it would be a miracle if she were to survive—especially in view of her enlarged heart. The damage had already been done in Zimbabwe and they questioned why it had taken me so long to bring her to South Africa. I hadn't expected to receive such terrible news—especially as the doctors hadn't even started treating her yet—and the impact of this just made me break down with uncontrollable tears. I fled to the toilets where I spent quite some time on the hard, cold floor as my sister tried to comfort me. Wendy helped me in so many other ways too and without her help during this awful time I probably would have had a nervous breakdown. The only thing that made me get up from that floor was the thought of Aida wondering where I had gone without telling her. I desperately wanted to keep her from worrying, so I washed my face and walked slowly back to the ward, praying that my little angel would not be able to see any of the signs of the distress that I felt. During all this, we had completely forgotten about Rosie in the little nursery next door. Luckily one of the wonderful nurses had taken charge and looked after her.

The stress of Aida being so ill took its toll on all of us. As I stood by her bed for hour after hour during that dark time, I would look at her lying there looking back at me with those big, beautiful eyes and her delightful smile of innocence, and it made me feel weak. The weakness raced through my body so that even standing up was difficult. I always had to have something to lean on and my heart would pound with fear. Whenever I held her or kissed her I would always try to smell that special fragrance of hers. Deep in my heart I was asking God, 'Why my little girl, why?' It was all like an appalling, nasty dream.

The doctors started their tests immediately rather than waiting until the next day, so I was happily relieved that they were trying to help Aida without delay. By the next day they had all their results and knew where to start. They decided to try to make her stronger and healthier in preparation for the operation and also to insert a shunt near her heart that would take out the fluid that was collecting and drain it into bags attached to her. These were collected regularly and disposed of when full. In less than a week, you could see a complete change in my daughter. Her eyes cleared, there was not as much swelling and her hair had started to grow back. She even developed a little appetite. Her diarrhoea had not stopped completely but it was certainly not as bad as it had been, although I think her stomach lining had been seriously affected. She also began to talk a lot to the doctors and nurses and was making lots of friends once again with her cheerful disposition. To help to relieve the boredom for her, I would take Aida around the hospital in a wheelchair visiting the various kiosks and other wards where she had made lots of friends.

A week later the shunt was still working with no problems. To see her whole being changing was so beautiful. She was getting healthier by the day as she ate a little more and her hands and legs were not so stiff anymore. Even with all this hope, the doctors still continued to call me to one side and repeat those awful words—that my daughter was dying and only a miracle would save her. Every time I was forced to face this, my sister would have to help me to the toilet where I would lie down on the cold, dirty floor and cry bitterly. Although I tried to hide my distress and hopelessness from Aida, she still asked awkward questions from time to time. One day she said, 'Mommy, am I going to die? I know my body is getting stronger and soon I will start walking again, but in case something happens to me, I have accepted Jesus into my life and I know he will look after me while I wait for you to come.' This broke my heart. She knew she was improving but had also accepted that she was going to die. Yet again, I rushed to the toilet and cried on the floor. This became a regular habit for me. If I was not at Aida's bedside, the nurses knew that they could find me in the toilet either vomiting or crying. When I had got myself together, as always I returned to my precious daughter's bedside. I would give her, her one hundred kisses, which she would count one by one in case I missed a few.

My sister Wendy and I had got into a routine. We'd get up at five in the morning and then make the long journey to the hospital, with me carrying a sleepy little Rosie in my arms. Usually we would go by bus, but sometimes Wendy's husband would be able to take us in his car. One thing never changed—our fear of what we would find at the hospital. On one occasion we arrived there and as we made the long walk down the corridor of the Renal Unit, we could see a crowd of doctors and nurses clustered together near Aida's ward, some of them crying. Of course, I instantly thought that my beloved daughter had passed away. Holding Rosie closely to me I ran, crying, straight to Aida's room but I stopped as I found out what they were crying about. Aida was sitting up in a wheelchair, singing a birthday song for a little boy called Arnold. It was his first birthday. I was so happy and relieved that I was forced to dash to the ladies room once again to hide my tears. But this time I was crying with joy. From that day on the doctors and nurses started to bring presents for Aida every day. I used some of the money donated by her friends at High School to buy her a television set. She had her favourite channels and shows and loved watching the television, so it brought her a lot of pleasure. Our life together during the day was becoming better, as we used to go on long walks with me pushing her in her wheelchair. At times we would sneak something small but tasty to snack on and we would giggle like schoolgirls, afraid we would get caught. Wendy would spend most of her time in the nursery looking after Rosie, leaving me time to spend with Aida. Every day there were stories in the newspapers about Aida's condition, as people seemed to want to know how she was getting on. These stories frequently mentioned the damage that had been done to her at the hospital in Zimbabwe.

The doctors were very pleased—and surprised—with the progress Aida was making. They couldn't believe the enormous improvement in her general condition in the short time she had been in hospital. One of the doctors even told me that they might consider a kidney transplant soon. This news made my excitement bubble up inside me; I felt so hopeful for the first time in ages. I suddenly thought that I would fly back to Zimbabwe to see my other children. I needed to see that they were OK and had money to pay the rent and so on. I needed to get everything in order ready for the big day of the transplant. I took Rosie with me and flew back the next day and found that all was well, with my children still being taken care of so well by my very good friends. I decided to spend the night there and fly straight back to South Africa the next day. I was so tired from the journey that I fell asleep in minutes, thinking that at least there was some hope for Aida now.

The next morning—25th August 1987—I got up just after 5 a.m. and sat down next to the phone. I just knew that it was going to ring. I had a sense that something was wrong but inside I refused to believe that it could be anything connected with Aida. I sat perfectly still, staring at the receiver, until it finally rang just after 7 a.m. At this point I suddenly knew, in my heart, that my child was dead. I just about managed to lift the receiver before I fell to the floor, clutching the phone, and crying so loudly that everyone in the house rushed to my side. The doctor was still on the other end of the phone and he was desperately trying to counsel me but I was on the floor screaming 'Where is my Jesus now?' so I heard nothing. I blamed myself for not being at her bedside. I did not say goodbye to her. I should never have come back to Zimbabwe.

After a while I found the strength to tell my family what had happened. I found out later that the cause of death was probably due to congestive cardiac failure. We arranged a flight back to South Africa for Rosie and me late that afternoon so that I could rush, as soon as possible, to my child's side. My daughter was far too young to die—only fourteen—and I thought many times during that bleak plane journey that I would have many, many questions to ask my Jesus when we met eventually, face to face. I found it all very difficult to accept but came to the conclusion that God only loans you his special child. He teaches you how to love each other and then he takes it all away from you without any explanation.

When I arrived in Johannesburg, my sister and brother-in-law were there to meet me but I can't remember how I got to the hospital. What I do remember is running, running through the corridor leading to my daughter's room and thinking that I would never get there. But when I did get there, all I saw was an empty bed. Even the sheets had gone. This must have made it all seem more real to me because I just fell to the floor, crying, 'Why, why?' One of the doctors picked me up and took me to one side of the room. He started trying to comfort me but I wasn't listening to a word he said. I think I was starting to become delirious at this stage as I imagined I was with Aida, running through a field, playing. I really believed I was with her but after some minutes had passed I began to realise, like waking from a dream, the truth. I knew my daughter had gone to heaven and that I would meet her again because she had said she would be waiting for me to come—and I believed her. I *had* to. All this time Rosie had been with my sister and the doctors who eventually came and took me down to the mortuary.

I had Rosie in my arms as I entered the mortuary building but I suddenly felt so weak that I almost dropped her and Wendy stepped forward just in time and took her from me. Rosie, of course, had no idea what was going on. I felt peculiar as we looked around and I wondered where they were keeping my child. I felt an ice-cold fear and emptiness. At the far end of the mortuary, the attendant opened a long drawer. In this cold, impersonal drawer lay my precious, beautiful angel—my Aida. I stepped forward, feeling all eyes on me as I pulled down the zip of the plastic body bag that covered her little body. All I could see was my little 'Sunshine' looking as if she were sleeping. I don't remember much, but I did notice that her hair had been growing back and had begun to cover the scar on her head from her operation. I bent forward and kissed my wonderful daughter gently on the forehead and then ever so lightly on her cold lips. Her tiny hands were crossed together as if she were trying to pray, still holding her green rosary and I was touched to see that she still had her little orange diamond 'wedding ring' upon her finger. Seeing her was the hardest thing to bear. I would have given anything to have been able to change places with her. I could only cry, stare at my beloved daughter and wonder why God had done this to us.[1]

---

1. See the Epilogue for a copy of a letter written by Aida to her mother the day before she died, and the Appendix for an extract from a statement by the doctor in charge of Aida's treatment at the time leading up to her death.

I travelled to Johannesburg Airport in the hearse, with Aida in her coffin and Rosie in my arms, leaving my sister and her family to follow behind in their car. I couldn't believe this was happening to me, it all seemed unreal, so when I came up against a problem at the airport check-in I almost gave up. At the desk the lady just said to me, 'Sorry, you cannot leave. Your ticket has not been paid for in Zimbabwe.' I thought that my family back in Zimbabwe, who controlled the funds, had made all the arrangements and payments for me. Hearing this, I simply sat down and cried. Once again I was left with nothing I could do except cry and ask why. I prayed to Jesus, 'Please Jesus help me. You have taken my child. What must I do now?' I was afraid the plane would leave soon—without us. An old Asian man appeared out of the crowd who was milling around me. He asked me gently why I was crying and, after I had told him my story, he took out his chequebook and made all the arrangements for our travel. He even notified people in Zimbabwe that there should be a hearse waiting for us when we landed and also let my family know that we were on our way. This was like a fairy tale. Where this angel came from I will never know, but in my heart I knew I was not alone. This was the second time Jesus had sent these angels to help me and yet again it had been an Asian gentleman. Everybody else had just passed me by, some staring at me as if I were a mad woman and others ignoring me completely. Maybe some people cannot be bothered with someone else's problems.

On the plane journey I could hardly think of anything other than my poor little daughter lying all alone in the cargo bay of the aircraft and this made me feel sick and would start me crying yet again. The airhostess had taken Rosie from me while I remained helpless in my seat, staring out at the huge white clouds that hung in the sky. I almost expected Aida to jump out of these clouds like an angel, saying, with that sweet little voice of hers, 'Mommy, where are my one hundred kisses?' I think at this point I was going delirious again. But I had to come back to the real world as we arrived back in Harare. I saw people moving about the plane and realised that now I had to take care of my child and I pushed forward. We were met by my two aunties—my mother's sisters Margaret and Violet—who were waiting with a big black hearse. We all kissed and then got into the car, with me holding Rosie on my lap and carrying Aida's little television set that she had loved so much. Aida's coffin was placed gently in the back of the hearse and we set off. We hadn't gone very far when my Auntie Margaret asked me why I had bought a television set for my child. She said it was wasting money that I would now need to settle accounts with. I just answered quietly that I had done it because it was what I wanted for my daughter but I began to cry and inside I was angry, thinking how horrible and penny pinching she sounded, when in a few days time I would be burying my beloved daughter.

Aida's funeral service was held at Braeside Church in Harare. The service and committal were conducted by Father Thomas who had baptised me, made my first Holy Communion, married me, married my parents, buried my mother and baptised Aida. And now he was burying Aida.

At the church I could not pay attention to the service. All I could think of was once again running and playing with my little girl. The time in the church flew past and now it was time to go and bury her. My family escorted me to the grave which was at the Warren Hills cemetery about eight miles away. (It was the same cemetery where Ighsan was buried, but I never gave him a second thought in my grief even though he was Aida's father.) People were standing all around, with Father Thomas by my side praying. I think this is when I finally realised that I was never, ever going to see my beautiful child again. I fell to my knees crying by the side of the grave and lay there thinking of jumping into that hole and giving Aida her last one hundred kisses goodbye. I had ripped open my stockings as I fell, cutting and bruising both my legs and after she had been laid to rest I had to be helped back to the car—I had lost all power in my legs. We all returned to Auntie Violet's house, as she had arranged some refreshments for the family. I just staggered to my room and lay there thinking that God had now taken away almost everyone I loved and that must be what he wanted.

Aida—my Sunshine (1973–1987)

13

Another marriage

In the morning I decided that we would go home straight away, but I had one important job to attend to before we left. I had to make sure that all the remaining money that had been donated to Aida was withdrawn from my auntie's account and handed over to someone else who desperately needed the money to pay for an operation. This was an old friend of mine from high school—a man called Enoch, who was married with four children. He had been in South Africa for seven years and had already had two kidney transplants, both of which his body had rejected. The money that had been collected for a transplant for my daughter might be able to pay for Enoch's third operation. I handed the money over to him with tears in my eyes and saw that he also was on the verge of tears. When they heard about this, Auntie Violet and Auntie Margaret were very cross, saying the money could have been used by me to pay my accounts. I refused, saying once again, 'God gave me these hands, I will use them.' I thanked them all for all their help with all the arrangements and left with my children for home in Gweru.

After about a month I applied for my old job back and they were so happy that I came back to work. But even working all day did not stop me thinking about Sunshine every second of my life and this would always bring instant tears to my eyes. When I got home in the evenings I would send someone to buy me some beer that I would drink until I fell asleep. Some days I didn't make it into work because of the awful hangovers I would get. I also started smoking and began to feel that my life was a complete mess. It seemed that all the people I love have to die and I wondered who was next.

I had finally written a letter to my fiancé explaining all that had happened to me and my daughter. He said that he had read it in the newspapers in Australia and that he had been trying to contact me for a long time. In all the upheaval and upset caused by Aida's illness I had not given him my change of telephone number. After I had given him my new phone number he phoned me about once or twice a month asking me to return to Australia. I felt I could not leave Aida in Zimbabwe and asked him to come to me, but he refused, saying he could not renew his contract in Zimbabwe. He also felt that the conditions were getting worse in the country. I felt rejected and hurt, as I needed him by my side to help me get over the pain of losing Aida. Not only had I lost my daughter, I had now lost my future husband and the chance of a new life in Australia with my family.

A few weeks later I decided to take my daughter Rosie for a short break to my Auntie Margaret's place in Bulawayo. I caught the kombi (a 12-seater minibus) for transport and we had just reached the outskirts of Bulawayo when the kombi front passenger door flew open and I tumbled out onto the main road holding Rosie in my arms. All I remember feeling was a rush of wind as we hurtled towards the road; then I found myself lying in the road with blood streaming down from the cuts to my head. My face was badly bruised, I had to have stitches in my neck and some fingers were broken, but I never let go of Rosie, who didn't even get a scratch on her! I was taken to the hospital in Bulawayo by ambulance to be patched up and was discharged later that same day, a shaken, battered survivor. Needless to say, we travelled the rest of the way to Auntie Margaret's by taxi. I felt very strange as we resumed our journey—as though this had not happened to me at all but that I had read about it in a newspaper. It was a peculiar and frightening experience but a miracle that Rosie came through unscathed. It certainly shook me up.

Just after this I heard that Enoch (whom I had helped with the money for a kidney transplant operation) had died. I think this news also made me go into my own world of depression and I continued to drink and smoke heavily. I just didn't seem to be able to shake off my feelings of hopelessness.

It was about three months after I buried my daughter that I met a man in a supermarket while I was doing some shopping for the children, in my drunken state. He was kind to me at this vulnerable time and we started a relationship. In 1988 I fell pregnant with my fifth child. This came as something of a surprise as I had not planned to have any more children. But I felt very happy to bring another baby into the world. It had been almost five years since I had had my last child, so being pregnant made me feel young again. When I got this news from the doctor I wondered what I should do. I decided that my baby would need a father figure and that if the baby's father, Kizito (known as Cris), wanted to marry me, I would say yes. I was just on the verge of telling him the news when he asked me to marry him. Without even thinking, I said yes.

We got married at Gweru Registry Office with most of my family not attending, as they did not approve of my choice of husband. There were just a few people at the wedding reception, my new husband's friends, who were drinkers just like him and looked like they had come for a quick booze up and not to bless our wedding at all. This was when I realised what a mistake I had made. I was filled with panic but, with nobody to turn to, I just said a silent prayer and decided to be strong for my unborn child and turn this new husband into somebody special. That was the biggest mistake I had ever made. I suppose I just wanted someone to love me and take over all these burdens that I felt I had carried alone for too long. Cris was the kind of husband who loved booze and music. When my father asked me why had I married this man, I was unable to answer him—because I didn't know myself. The mistake was mine and I knew it, but I would never divorce him but do everything possible to make a go of things.

When the reception was over I felt so guilty but I could not explain why. Maybe I knew that my love for him was not real—like the love I had for Ighsan. The guilt made me feel that I had to return to see my late ex-husband's grave. I took a bus journey all the way from Gweru to the Warren Hills cemetery in Harare. On arrival my tears started to fall while I looked for the Muslim section of the cemetery, only to find that nobody had looked after his grave. I fell down on my knees and pulled out each and every weed with my tears falling down on his grave. When I had finished it was the cleanest grave in the cemetery. Before leaving I sang our song 'Close to You' and said a prayer.

In the same cemetery, our daughter Aida was also buried, so after tending to Ighsan's grave I made my way through to my little Sunshine's grave. I saw the little white angel headstone I had placed and this looked so human that I cried even more than ever for my little girl. Not knowing what to do next, I threw myself beside the grave and started praying and telling her everything is going to be alright and that I would look after her two sisters and her brother and make sure that we would all meet in heaven one day. After I had finished my prayers and my little 'chat' with Aida, I realised an expensive dome made out of flowers had been stolen from her grave. It made me so sad that anybody would want to steal from a resting place for people that had passed away. As I walked away from the cemetery I felt at least a little bit better than before, knowing that I had just spoken to two of the most precious people in my world and I do know that I was heard. It was so good being alone at last, able to think quietly. As I made my way back through all the graves, I sang a song my daughter had liked, hoping that where she was she was listening.

In the months that followed, my husband, Cris, drank all the time and I hardly saw him. He was always making deals for money in the pubs or in some alleyway. I had no idea whether he was faithful or not and this made me worry so much because people in Zimbabwe were dying of AIDS every day. Wherever you walked around the town you would always see someone with AIDS. I think that one of the reasons for this was that the men were allowed to have more than one wife. In fact, my grandfather on my father's side (who I hardly knew) had eight wives including one in Britain. Five of his wives were from one family and the others were cousins.

On one occasion when my husband was at home and sober, I asked him whether it was possible for us to pool our money, so that maybe we could think of buying a house. I thought this would be the best thing to do because the rent was so high in the town. I thought we could also sink a borehole because at that time in Zimbabwe there was a drought. We were only allowed to use water at certain times of the day and the water bills were always high. The only response I got from him was that it was impossible for him to save. Rather than sending me deeper into my depression as might have been expected, this spurred me into action. At this point I felt that during the last fourteen years I had gained nothing for my children, so I decided to change things. I decided to have a drink just once a week, not to allow anybody to smoke in front of my children and to work hard for the good of my children. I turned myself into a workaholic, making money for my children to live properly and have good food on the table.

With this last pregnancy I felt so well, happy and energetic, planning for the baby—I didn't even get any morning sickness. I waited and waited but the due date came and went. Eventually I was admitted to the Birchenough Maternity Hospital where the labour was to be induced by inserting a drip, but when the nurse examined me she said that there was no heartbeat. The doctor was out of town doing his own thing and he told the nurse to rush me to Gweru Hospital for a Caesarean birth. There was no time to wait, so out came the drip and I was bundled into an ambulance. I was so upset and worried—not for my life but that my baby was dead in my stomach. My husband was nowhere around and I was alone again as I cried.

I was prepped for theatre but there was no doctor available just then. They brought in an old retired doctor to help but she looked as if she couldn't see properly and she made a very crooked incision and I think she stitched the cut very badly as I'm left with a thick, ugly scar to this day.

I awoke from the operation crying with the thought that I had lost my child, but as I looked to my side there was a tiny cot with a beautiful baby boy inside—my son Christopher, born in January 1989. He had red cheeks and black hair and looked like a little angel sleeping. I cried and cried, even worse than before when I had thought him dead, but now I was the happiest mother in the world. I picked up my beautiful son and already felt that we had been made for each other. I put him to sleep next to me—it felt like heaven. My son Shane and my husband walked in at that point to wish me congratulations. They both kissed me and said over and over again that our new baby was so beautiful. They didn't stay long though, as my husband said he had something he urgently wanted to see to.

After a while I told the nurse that I would like to use the toilet but she just simply told me to get up and go myself. I was still feeling weak and sore from the operation but I managed to make my way to the toilet, lamely holding my stomach, shuffling along, without help. When I got there I was appalled by the sight that met me. I rang the bell, complaining of how dirty the toilets were. They were filthy and smelly and the seat was full of blood. The nurse came in and shouted at me. She said I was a proud woman and that she was not going to clean the seat. I was so upset that I simply walked back to my bed, bundled up my baby and left. I went to the hospital office and phoned a taxi and was soon back at home with my son Shane tucking me up nicely into my bed.

After a couple of days resting I decided to go for a bath on my own. In the bathroom I fell to the floor and when Shane picked me up I began to bleed huge clots of blood that covered the whole floor. It was only with my son's help that I was able to bath and change and get back into bed—with some tablets for the pain. After a few days of this the doctor came and removed all my stitches and I was able to move around more freely. Shane was a huge help to me but my husband was always too busy seeing to his things that he couldn't spare much time for me or the children.

When Christopher was about three months old he suffered a breathing problem. It was strange—when he was asleep on the bed he struggled to breathe, but when I was holding him in my arms he breathed quite well. I took him to the doctors but all they did was prescribe antibiotics. This carried on until he was three years old and every day during this time I would hold him in my arms while he slept each and every day. I became so exhausted that I asked my doctor to refer me to a specialist. We found one in Harare and we went there against my husband's wishes. I just had to go against him to look after my child.

The specialist examined Christopher and told us that he had some skin growing through his nostrils that was interfering with his breathing. They decided to remove this and, at the same time, remove his tonsils because of the trouble they gave him. I stayed in the hospital with him and can remember my happiness and joy as they wheeled him out of the operating theatre. His little cheeks were so rosy and flushed. His eyes were wide open and he spoke to me straight away, saying, 'Mommy, can I have some ice cream?' I ran for the ice cream and was so happy to see him eat it with no trouble and without spitting too much blood out. Soon after I was able to take my baby home again, knowing that this time we were both going to get some sleep.

When I was well again I decided to go back to work for money reasons—my husband didn't do much for us—and got a job at the Ministry of Health. The situation in Zimbabwe was deteriorating all the time and at work things were getting ugly now because there were too many people stealing. People stole old clothing meant for the poor, soap and meat meant for the hospital, boots and dustcoats meant for the workers, tablets meant for the sick, and all sorts of other things that went missing. The first person that would come under suspicion for all these thefts was the poor mixed race person—me. I was so afraid that I did what other people did before me and put my notice in and collected my pension. I had to take action before I found myself in jail for something I hadn't done.

My chicken business still carried on and we were making good money and managing to put some in the bank every week. Added to my pension this amounted to a fair amount of money so I decided to open my first shop to be called 'Janey's'. It was going to be a café and a takeaway selling *sadza* with beef stew, and cows' hooves that the men folk truly loved. They used to say that this would increase their potency with women. My shop was in a good spot—it was situated in-between three beer halls—so when the men finished drinking they all came to me for breakfast, lunch and supper. Gweru train station was next door so the people waiting would also come in for a meal. We stayed open till late at night and did so well that within a few months I caught the train to South Africa and bought my first car—a red, second-hand Renault 5. My family was totally shocked by this. Soon Shane was begging me for us to take the chicken business more seriously. He could see the potential and the possible rewards. We worked day and night selling chickens to anyone and everyone—even to the people who worked in the banks. We got so many customers that I saved up the deposit for a house. When I told my husband, who was not working, he did not believe me. So, when I bought a beautiful house with a swimming pool (from a man who needed only cash to pay for his hospital bill, so the rest of the money was on deed of sale), the papers were all signed in my maiden name. When I got the keys to this wonderful property it gave my family a real surprise—including my husband.

Janey's Café

Things were all going so smoothly that year with Christopher growing so nicely without any more problems, my children all happy and me prospering with my shop and other things, but then my health started to give me problems. Suddenly I began to have pains in my stomach so I made an appointment to see a doctor, only to be told that I was about three months pregnant. What could I do but accept this and try to make the best of the situation? My husband was extremely happy when I broke the news and he decided to take us all for a day out. The trip he chose was to a mountainous rural area called Chiwundura. You had to travel along dirt roads to get there and, not thinking there was any danger, I agreed.

For the journey I packed some food and water for the children, some tea in a flask for me and cold beers for my husband. The day was very dry and hot with hardly any breeze blowing. It took hours on end before we reached our destination. When we got there I was so disappointed as I had thought it would be something more comfortable, with more to see, but I tried to go along with his enthusiasm. We all sat in the car and ate the nice home-cooked meal I had packed and we laughed and talked as my husband quietly drank his beers. When he had finished them all he insisted we went to find more, so by the time we were on the way home it was dark. We spent an hour trying to find the right route and my husband's driving deteriorated dramatically because he was drunk. We were so exhausted and stressed when we eventually arrived home that we just collapsed onto the sofa rather than in our bed.

Me and my Father with Jane, Rosie and Christopher

When I roused myself from the sofa I had a quick bath and shortly after that I started getting pains low down in my stomach and a bit of a discharge. I took two tablets for the pain and prepared for bed, but the pain got worse and there was a sudden flow of blood. I began to panic and the children were so worried that they tried to wake up my husband. When he didn't get up I decided to catch a taxi to town. When we reached the hospital I was rushed to the emergency room, bleeding heavily. The doctor scheduled me for a D&C (Dilation and Curettage) to clean out my womb as I had just had, he informed me, a miscarriage.

The next day my husband arrived with a bad hangover just as I was being wheeled into theatre for my operation. Although at this point I was questioning why I had gone out for that drive with him, why he had driven over so much rough ground and why he had drunk so much, I knew I had to put it out of my mind and carry on with my life as if nothing had happened. I was determined that this time I would not make any more mistakes; there would be no more babies. I knew that I would have to fight to look after my children and my businesses and I also knew that I was ready to do it.

Married life

After recovering from my miscarriage, we moved into our beautiful house. It had four bedrooms, a dining room, a kitchen, bathroom, toilet and a very large pantry. Some of the rooms had carpets and were fitted with large wardrobes and beautiful fireplaces. Outside were two cottages in which I had lodgers. Next to the pool there was a very large chicken run, built like a house—something people could live in. All this was on a two-acre stand.

Christopher graduating from nursery

I decided to build a wooden kitchen with a firewood stove like the kind we had had with my granny, so that I could cook outside and it would also be useful for the preparation of the chickens for our business. By now this business consisted of buying approximately 100 whole chickens and 500 chicken heads from nearby farms every other day, all of which had to be plucked, cleaned and dressed ready for sale the next morning to the waiting customers. The heads were sold ten at a time for one dollar and made a very good meal eaten with *sadza*. On a daily basis we would also buy one or two large cow's heads. These would be cleaned and cut up with an axe and put into big pots to boil until soft. This was then sold at the shop to the beer hall drinkers. Later I imported day-old broilers from Britain—the real parent stock—and grew them till they were on the point of laying. I then incubated my own day-old chicks for sale. I also grew some of them until they were six weeks old and ready for sale. By this time, my chicken run was divided into four different sections with four different age groups and when I was in the run it felt like heaven—that's how I loved my birds. All this time the business was growing and I was always looking for ways to make more money from the chickens and from the food I made. I even became the Shurugwi authorised agent for 'Stewarts Day Old Chicks'—an agency supplying broiler and laying chicks—based in Chegutu, which is about 90 miles west of Harare. The chicks would arrive at Gweru railway station on Wednesdays and Saturdays and I would collect them in my pickup and then prepare them for sale.

The shop was doing so well that we opened another one. This was in the town where I was born, Shurugwi, near my grandfather's farm, and we sold second-hand furniture, groceries and meat to the local people and to all the miners in that area. The older people used to call me 'Jimmy's child' after my grandfather. The meat I would buy as a whole cow, which was then slaughtered, cleaned and cut up into pieces at the farm and transported back to my house for packing ready to sell in my shops. When I could get them, I would also buy week-old calves. The skins from the calves were sold to the Bata Shoe factory in Gweru. Another little business venture that I had going was that about once a month we would fill up my truck with second-hand clothes and furniture that I bought from the auctions held by the Gweru Police. These were goods that had been stolen and recovered but nobody had claimed. We would park up in a township and in about two hours everything would be sold. Many times I would get to bed at 2 a.m. feeling utterly exhausted but very satisfied with my work.

It became very difficult for me to travel every day on top of all the other things I had to do such as taking stock once a month or delivering meat and furniture so I got someone to run the business for me and sometimes my daughter, Nippy, would help me. If I asked my husband for help with the driving he would ask to be paid by me buying beer the whole way there and back and making sure we stopped at each pub.

During a trip to one of my shops in Shurugwi to deliver some second-hand furniture, I got so dizzy and sick that I felt like vomiting. I returned home as quickly as I possibly could, because I thought a lie down would do the trick. On arrival home my son Christopher, then aged 7, tucked me up into bed. I was now vomiting very frequently and had diarrhoea, which left me very dehydrated and I soon became incapable of driving or walking. Thinking there must be something badly wrong with me, I had to send my young son to town to look for a taxi to take me to the hospital as there was no one else at home and the telephone was out of order. All I could do was lie there and worry about my son. The journey was about 10 miles and I worried that something might happen to him along the way. He was all alone on the main road and I prayed to Jesus to guide him. After a few hours my wonderful son returned with a taxi and, with the help of the driver, I climbed in the back and laid myself down on some pillows. He then drove us to the hospital. All the way I was vomiting blood, feeling dizzy and had a high temperature and my son was at my side saying, 'Mommy, I would have come back sooner but nobody wanted to listen to me. They all thought I was playing.' At the hospital I was taken out on a stretcher and into the emergency room where a doctor examined me. After a few minutes, the doctor said that I had been poisoned but he did not know by what as yet. With this he started to put me on a drip straightaway but he struggled. He was pricking me all over as my veins had collapsed by this time but eventually he managed. The doctor said that my son's prompt action had saved my life because if I had been a few hours later getting to the hospital I would have died. Later that evening I began to feel well again. At 2 a.m. the following morning my husband marched in to visit me (even though he had been informed at 4 p.m. the previous day). He was drunk and looked as if he had just come off the washing line. On seeing the state he was in I just asked him politely to leave me to rest and I cried myself to sleep thinking that all I had tonight was my Jesus and my son who got me to the hospital. I will never know who or what had poisoned me. I just stored it all away in my head, like all the other secrets I kept all these years.

My brother Harry with Christopher

Shortly after this frightening episode, my health gave me problems yet again. I had been experiencing stomach pains and diarrhoea for some time but decided not to see a doctor as I thought it was nothing that could kill me and that it would soon pass. It was on a beautiful Sunday morning after I had just come back from church, when suddenly I had these sharp pains in my stomach. I ran to the toilet screaming with the pain and spent at least an hour in there crying and feeling that I was going to die. I crawled to my room to change and then went to see my doctor. On arrival at my doctor's he hurriedly examined me and I was rushed to the Mater Dei private hospital in Bulawayo for an emergency operation. My gall bladder had gallstones and was about to burst. I had to have it removed completely as it was so bad and he asked why I had not been to see him before then. When I arrived at the hospital I could no longer walk and I was taken by wheelchair to the maternity ward by mistake, as my stomach was so big. When I got there I was told to undress and put on a gown and, as I was doing this, the nurse was putting on some rubber gloves to see how many centimetres my cervix was dilated. As sick as I was I had to cry. I had come in with a gall bladder problem and was being prepped to give birth! I soon found my way to the correct ward when I managed to tell the shocked nurse what the real problem was. I was soon seen by a specialist who ordered a major operation immediately and warned that my family should be informed, together with a priest. When my husband, family and priest arrived I went into the operating theatre and the last thing I thought was that I would be able to see my little 'Sunshine' again. After some hours I awoke feeling dizzy and wondering where I was. The doctor had given me some morphine and I think that made me feel as if I was in the clouds, not comprehending what had happened to me. After I realized that I was not dead and that Jesus had given me time to look after my family, I was so happy to be alive that I prayed. When the doctor walked in smiling I knew that all was well. He handed me a small Vaseline jar full of little yellow gallstones and told me that my gall bladder had had so many of these that it would have burst if he hadn't removed it. With a feeling of happiness that there would be no more pain, I just fell into a deep sleep. After a few days I was discharged from the hospital and went back to my family, which was so glorious to me. The removal of my gall bladder causes me to get a lot of acid, and I find drinking bottled soda water gives me relief.

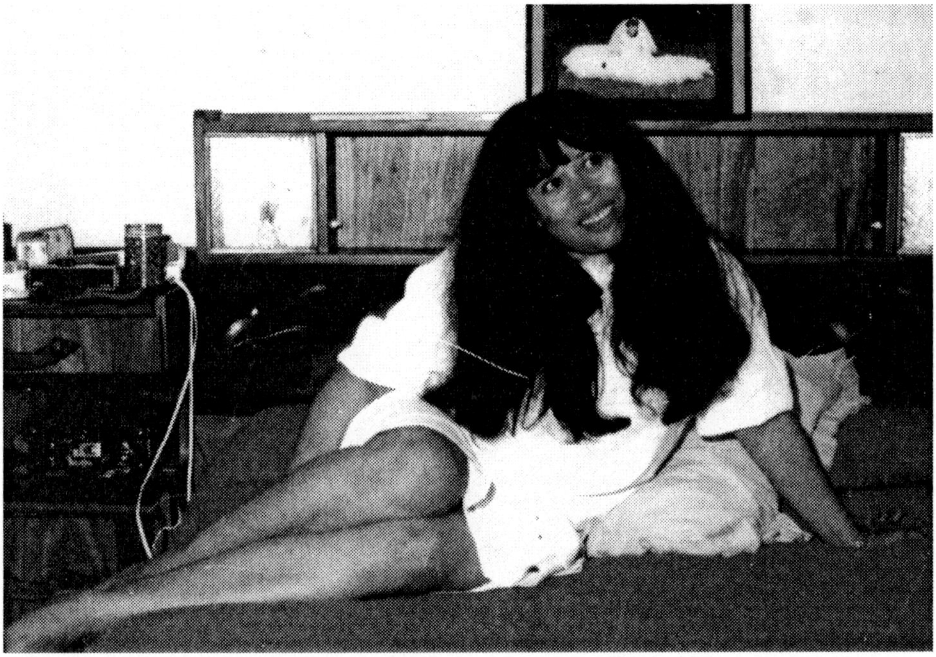

Pregnant with Christopher

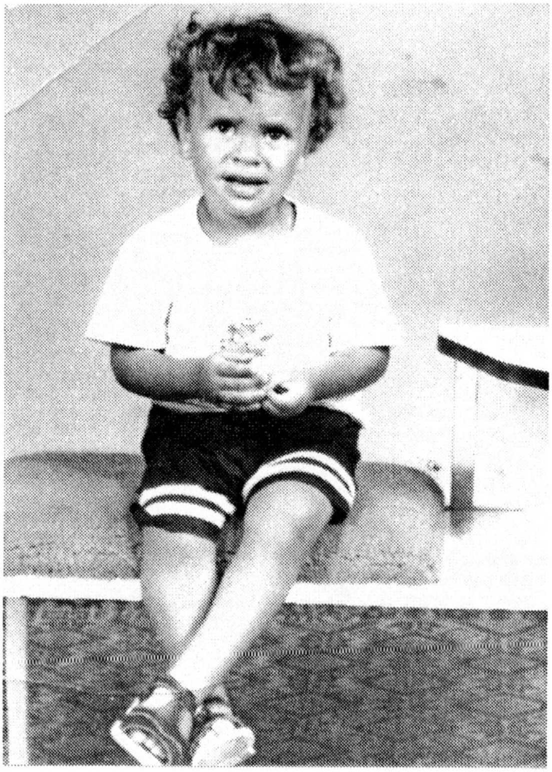

Christopher

14

Deciding to leave Zimbabwe

Whenever we had any problems in our lives my husband would get out of hand, using violence and abusive language on me. I tried to report this to the police but when they asked his name they knew straight away that it was their friend. They protected him, asking me why I didn't leave this black man alone and go stay in Britain. With this they just started laughing and I had to leave the police station, furious, and with my feelings so hurt. On many occasions my husband would be away from home overnight saying he was busy transporting people all over to earn money. I always suspected that he was sleeping with other women and felt that he did not care about my feelings at all. I would sometimes lock the doors, but this would only make matters worse, because when he did finally arrive home he would be banging on the door and shouting to be let in. This would wake up the children and eventually I would have to open the door to him. I thought that if I let him in, things would be all right, but he would start shouting and pushing me around. My daughter Rosie was the only one brave enough to stand in front of him and try to protect me by holding up her little fists. Seeing this reminded me of myself as a young girl, trying to protect my own mother from my father. The same thing was happening again. My husband would simply push Rosie aside and rush towards me smacking me in the face. I would fall on the floor hard, covered with blood, with Rosie looking down at me, crying. With this he would just walk away and relax in a different part of the house. To this day I have a lump on the back of my head where I fell on the floor. Every now and again it gives me so much pain and I have sleepless nights. In my heart I always knew my husband had something to do with all the pain and sufferings that I went through because he was very jealous of me and tried to kill me so many times. Once he even connected some wires to the car battery and when I drove the car, the bonnet went up in smoke and the engine would not turn off, resulting in the car just running and running. I then drove to my son Shane's place of work and he knew exactly how to switch off the engine. Sometimes my husband would deliberately drive straight into some trees, causing us some injury. At other times, he would take battery acid, which he used for cleaning his cars, and would threaten to throw this into my face so nobody would ever look at me again. Even though I knew that all these things were mad, I thought of my youngest son who loved his father, so I tried to stay on with my marriage, thinking one day he would change.

Later I decided to open a little kiosk by the side of my house so I went to the city council and they approved this. I paid money for a builder and bought all that was needed, which was very expensive. All my children helped me to clean the area, and then we called in our builder. He was just pegging out the area ready to start building, when we saw the city council man coming back to tell me that I was on the wrong area zone. Eventually, they gave me another area for the kiosk, which was also near my house. But once again when building started they stopped me. They said this time that the neighbours next door didn't want a kiosk near them. Yet again we were given another area to clean. It was more difficult this time as there were thorn trees and big bushes on the site. Our hands were all full of blisters by the time we had finished clearing the site. All together this happened five times, with different excuses why I couldn't have the site, until I was given a kiosk in town. They made me renovate this whole place, painting and putting up new shelves. I bought fridges and put in a stove for cooking and felt that at long last I had managed to get everything going well. This place catered for all sorts of people, mostly the police and war veterans.

At this time a lot of trouble started going on in the area with the white farmers. The war veterans were targeting people who didn't belong to their party, killing some of the farmers, going into some people's houses and destroying all their livelihoods. People broke into our house on many occasions and my husband would be fast asleep (being drunk) so I handled everything on my own. At one time I even had to fight with a man standing in our house—this was so terrifying. On some occasions I would find all my chickens with their heads cut off and this made me stop keeping poultry altogether: it costs a lot of money to grow them and was disheartening to have them killed by some other person. This is when I started to hate Zimbabwe. To live in fear like this is devastating and I became more and more scared each day that one day they were going to kill my children. I also had to close the shop in Shurugwe because people were repeatedly breaking into it and stealing. When there was no petrol I had to catch a bus, so that returning home became such a problem. I was abused by drunken youths on the bus the whole way home.

Another business that I had was more unusual. My father had given me a nice little goldmine in Gweru that I called 'Favourite' because it was my favourite project. The workers used to produce 30 tons of ore that would have to be transported by truck to the mill in Shurugwe that produced the gold. The process, from digging out the ore to producing the piece of gold, would take one month; then the whole process would start again. But there were problems here, too. The black farmer whose land the mine was on threatened to shoot my workers for picking up dead wood to make a fire to cook their food on. The farmer would, from time to time, also take away their clothes and tie them naked to a tree. His actions were reported to the local police but no action was taken. This made me feel so afraid that after two years I sold the mine for a mere three thousand dollars.

With my businesses being targeted and my having to give up the poultry, the shops and the mine, I knew I had to do something different if I was going to continue to earn a good living for my family. With the money I got from selling the mine I decided to convert my house into a boys' hostel. This provided accommodation for boys aged 17–20 attending college in Gweru. The nineteen boys totally destroyed my house and within a year I had to close it down. I bought a house across the road until my own house was renovated.

I had also become afraid to be in my shop next to the pubs because some people used to ill-treat us, calling us names when they were drunk. One man actually spat in my daughter Nippy's face and made some very bad threats. The police did nothing about this. I wasn't the only person to suffer in this area. There was an old white lady, called Mary, who had an antiques shop next door to me. She helped everybody and looked after many of the poor people nearby. She was somebody I really loved and respected and every morning she would look for me just to say good morning. One Sunday, late in the afternoon, some men broke into her house and tied her with wire around her hands, and stabbed her in her neck after taking some money. When I heard this story my heart was so full of hatred that I closed that shop immediately, afraid I would be next.

My kiosk was still running nicely, with no problems, until one day I saw a city council car arrive. I somehow knew this meant trouble. The Engineering Services Department issued me with a letter giving me notice to say I was in the wrong area zone and to cease operating the kiosk. I went to the mayor for help but he only said that he did not interfere with the city council. The only thing he could do for me was to ask them if I could finish the month. Despite their agreement to this, before the month was up they came with a big chain and locked up the place with all my belongings and stock in the kiosk together with all the money and hard work I had invested gone to waste.

I wasn't the only one in my family to have troubles. My brother Kenny had married and his wife, Sandra, was almost nine months pregnant. On her last check up she was examined by the doctor and was given the awful news that the baby was dead. They induced labour and their poor, tiny dead baby was taken to the mortuary, wrapped in his little blue blanket. We had to go there and sort out the funeral arrangements but we found that the mortuary didn't have any coffins. We were told to find a small box to put the baby in and take the body to the hospital were it would be cremated. Of course, this is a terrible thing for anyone to have to do but things were about to get worse. When we arrived at the hospital with the baby in the nicest box we had been able to find, we were led to a little fireplace. It was like a small wooden stove and it was so public, with people walking up and down. We could hardly believe what we were seeing but this is where one of the nurses took the baby out of the box and laid him down on the top of the ashes. As a mother, I thought this was such a cruel thing for any husband and wife to witness but my brother and his heartbroken wife had to watch their son burn and turn into ashes in the fire. Surely, anybody with a heart wouldn't allow this.

Another secret I have kept all this time is that one of my daughters was raped and made pregnant by a war veteran's son. I reported the case to the police but they just laughed at us. Feeling ashamed, we looked for a doctor to help us. All they asked for was ten thousand dollars and the abortion would be carried out in an illegal clinic, which nobody knew about. This was done, but all the hurt and pain that I felt for my daughter added to what I was feeling about my country. I was now thinking about leaving Zimbabwe because I felt I—or someone from my family—would be next to be injured, abused or even killed.

Before I eventually left Zimbabwe I was determined to help a relative of mine who was dying of AIDS. Godfrey was one of my favourite cousins and was also one of the most wonderful people I had ever met. He was only in his early forties and was crippled, confined to a wheelchair. I never knew how he contracted the AIDS virus.

With my brother Kenny and my daughters Rosie and Nippy, I set off to say my goodbyes to Godfrey who lived in Bulawayo. As always in Zimbabwe it was a difficult journey. In preparation for leaving Zimbabwe I had sold my cars and property and now had no means of transport and the only way I could travel was to hire a taxi. This meant that I had to pay extra money for black market petrol, as there was no petrol to be had legally in Zimbabwe. The radio in the taxi was not working but the taxi driver had a single cassette tape of the Boyzone album 'By Request' which he played over and over again for the entire journey there and back. That music will always remind me of seeing Godfrey. On the way to Bulawayo we got lost and had a slight accident but nobody was hurt (only the front of the taxi was damaged) but we eventually found where Godfrey was staying.

When we got there I met his lovely family and was taken through to see him. I found myself staring at a skeleton dressed in skin and my tears began to flow. I think it made me think too much about my little Sunshine and the way she had looked towards the end with her hands curled up and her legs buckling inwards, just like a baby. All I could do was pray for him until I felt I could stay no longer without breaking down. The journey back to Gweru was very quiet. Kenny and I were lost in our own thoughts and the children had never seen someone in such a bad way before.

About a year later, when I was in Britain, I was informed of Godfrey's death. I was surprised to find that I wasn't too upset as I knew he was going to be taken good care of by our creator and there would be no more suffering. If only I could have believed this when my little Aida had been taken from me—but I couldn't, I was too angry.

In my quest to find a way to leave Zimbabwe, I met up again with a Zimbabwean friend called Tarero whom I had met several years ago as our children used to go to school together. She had left Zimbabwe and had returned for a short holiday from Ireland where she was now resident.

She was working in Dublin and told me how easy it would be for me to settle in Dublin. I could apply for a stay under ancestral rights, as one of my grandfathers was born in Ireland. It sounded so good that I jumped at the opportunity and gave Tarero a lot of money to look after for me. I had managed to change some money into pounds and I would collect it on my arrival in Ireland to pay for my expenses until I got settled. We exchanged addresses and phone numbers. After she returned to Ireland she wrote me a letter that I would show to the immigration officials on my arrival with her address and telephone number in case of a problem and she telephoned me twice, reassuring me that everything was alright. We were friends and I fully trusted her.

I went home that same day and discussed my plans with my husband before he went on his rounds, like a doctor, doing his dealing. I told him that I was leaving with my eldest daughter for Ireland, thinking he would fight me but he fully approved and even suggested that I sell my house and car leaving him with half of the money. He needed the money because he would be looking after my other two children, Rosie and Christopher, who were still living at home. At this point my first-born, Shane, was a grown man, married with three children. He had been working for a British company called Airwork Limited in Gweru, which had closed down and given him a small pension to live on. He was also a preacher at the local Pentecostal church in our little farm town. I sold my car and my beautiful house and got next to nothing for them because people in Zimbabwe had no money. After I gave my husband his share I had just enough money to buy two plane tickets to Ireland. I had to give away all my other belongings and my heart cried out for all my hard work. No matter what the sacrifice, I knew that I had to get out and start a new life. At this time I was still a very strong woman and could work very hard without giving up so I was confident of success even though I was worried about this new venture.

The plan was for my husband, plus Rosie and Christopher, to stay in Shane's house until I could make arrangements for them to join me in Ireland. I had many sleepless nights and kept thinking that perhaps I was doing the wrong thing—but it was too late to turn back now.

Christopher on a delivery bicycle

Christopher and Rosie just before they came to Britain

My husband, Cris, agreed to take Nippy and me to Harare Airport. I kissed, hugged and said goodbye to my children, telling them I would send for them immediately after I was settled. This was such a scary thing for me to do and made me tremble.

I cried all the way to the airport, thinking I would never get there in time for my flight as Cris kept stopping at each and every bar on the way. On arrival he was so drunk that I don't think he even remembered saying goodbye.

At the airport everyone looked like they knew what they were doing except me. My mind was just racing, looking at the plane that was going to take me away and I almost changed my mind as I thought this was the last time I would be on Zimbabwean soil.

15

A new life

The plane journey out of Zimbabwe was filled with all sorts of emotions. I couldn't help but look back and my thoughts dwelled on my children, my shops and how hard I had worked to make money. I felt a certain peace at putting all this behind me, but at the same time I felt like someone who was just like a robot waiting for the next thing to happen. I was so tired of my wasted years suffering from racial abuse and corruption in Zimbabwe that I was willing to try anything so that my children could have a better life and I was willing to die for this cause if necessary. I was on some special medication for draining fluid from my legs and also some tablets that one doctor had prescribed, telling me my heart was enlarged and that I would die without these tablets. He said I would have to take these tablets for the rest of my life so I carried a few months supply, which I thought would last me till I was settled.

We travelled the whole night on the airplane and I couldn't help but think about the children I had left behind and cried as I looked at my tired daughter next to me and wondered if I had made the right decision. I had severe pains in my stomach, started a migraine headache and had to vomit into an empty plastic bag I found.

We landed safely at Gatwick Airport to catch our connecting flight to Dublin on the 14th February 2001, but we had to go through Immigration first. Landing on British soil was so exciting to me. I had always dreamt of this moment and I felt relieved at this stage that I had made the right decision. I couldn't wait to get to Ireland and see a solicitor to sort out my children's future just as all my other family members had done before me. But first we had to deal with Immigration. Nippy and I looked around at all the people of different races, wearing different dress. The place we were walking into was something so beautiful to us that our jaws dropped in amazement as we walked to the Immigration lines. There were people of so many different races, dressed in colourful clothes. We all lined up with our passports and I somehow knew that there was going to be trouble ahead.

Even so, I was shocked when Immigration asked us where we were going. I explained that I was on my way to Dublin with my daughter to meet a friend. I gave them the letter I had received from Tarero with her address and telephone on. They went away to check the details of this friend, and they left us sitting there, worrying. When they came back they just briskly informed me that we had to return to Zimbabwe on the next available flight. They didn't say any more but what I think happened is that they phoned Tarero, the girl friend I was to stay with, and she must have said something to the immigration that caused them to disbelieve my story. I think maybe she did this because in Zimbabwe, when we made these arrangements, I had given her a lot of money. I wanted her to keep this for me in case the immigration people took it away from me. I was so used to the corruption in daily life in Zimbabwe that I really believed this would happen and so I chose to trust this friend. I know now not to trust even the closest friend. I realised at that moment that the friend I had given my money to in Zimbabwe had said something bad and caused this trouble for me. I began to cry uncontrollably, with a very different kind of fear that is very hard to explain.

All the people who were getting deported were escorted away by Immigration officers and police with dogs and then closed up in one room, with just one toilet and some chairs for sitting on. I couldn't believe we were being treated like this—I was not a criminal and had done nothing to deserve all this. My daughter took me to the toilet to calm me down but I started vomiting with the shock and also maybe with hunger as I hadn't eaten anything the previous day. There was no way in which I was going back after all the persecution I had suffered. I had to think fast. The next thing that came into my head was to say I wanted to declare asylum here in Britain so I began beating on the windows of the little room. A young policeman noticed that we were distressed and came to collect us. We were taken to another heavily guarded room to be questioned. They asked why I was changing my statement so I told the immigration that death was far better than to live another day in Zimbabwe. That same day Immigration officers fingerprinted us and took snapshots—just like we were criminals going to prison; then, several hours later, they escorted us to a huge bus. I was now totally convinced it was waiting to take us to a prison but we were not really informed where we were going. We just had to follow.

It was around three in the morning when we arrived at a place called Oakington Immigration Reception Centre in Longstanton, Cambridgeshire—a fast-track centre for asylum claims. We were searched thoroughly—a body search as well as our suitcases. All our documents were taken away including money. I was told that if I wanted any of my money, it would be given to me. By about 5 a.m.

we had been 'processed' and we were taken to a dormitory with bars on the windows and guarded with huge fences. Now I really thought we were in prison. I saw the beds all lined up in rows, with small, hard mattresses, a very hard pillow and an itchy brown blanket on each bed. This was in the wintertime and the heater near me was not working—but I was too scared to complain.

Every morning when I woke, the first thing I would see would be big black iron bars on the windows and beyond that the barbed wire fencing surrounding the centre, with officers 'protecting' us in case we wanted to escape or commit suicide. After the meals there was nothing else to do to occupy your mind, so I would just go back to my bed and lie there looking up at the window bars, hoping and praying that they would just disappear and sometimes even thinking that all this was just a very bad dream.

This was the beginning of my depression. For the first two days I had a migraine headache but when I went to the immigration doctor all they gave me was two tablets. I told him that I had brought my own medication for my heart and for my swollen legs and that if I didn't keep taking the tablets I was going to die and then who would take care of my children? For over four years I had taken these tablets and now they just threw the lot away. I just couldn't stop crying, thinking I was going to die. The doctors then sent me to a hospital for an x-ray on my heart and found nothing wrong with me. Another thing I noticed was that the swelling disappeared from my legs. The doctor just said that I must have been working too hard and that is why my legs would swell up. It was a shock to realise that I didn't need any of the drugs I had been prescribed in Zimbabwe.

At my first hearing in Oakington, my case was given a refusal. Maybe I had failed to express myself properly—I was so afraid of people, especially being in a strange place that looked like a prison. The solicitor we had said we had all the entitlement papers to stay in Britain. I had my grandfather's papers and I had other family members who were already staying in Britain with the same documents. The only thing missing was my grandfather's birth certificate. The following two and a half weeks were pure mental torture for me. I just spent all the time crying—day and night without stopping—and my eyes developed huge bags underneath them. All I could think about was that I was going to die and who was going to take care of my children.

Some of the guards were very nice but others were very cruel and didn't want you to even talk to them. They would say 'go back to sleep' whatever you said and even if you were in pain you were not given anything. We were also ill treated by some of the girls that were in the same dormitory. There were several who used to speak in their native language, obviously not aware that I too could speak their language. I knew that some of these girls would get their stay by telling lies because I could hear the things they talked about. I couldn't help but feel sorry for myself because telling the truth had got me nowhere. These girls reminded me of the country that I had just run away from. They were African racists, not wanting to know me or my daughter and yet they knew we came from the same place.

I gave a relative's address to my solicitors and they asked me if I wanted to be released to that address. I agreed and we caught a train from Cambridge for Birmingham. I was given my money and other documents back, but not our passports. I was informed that there would be no support because I had my own money. I told them that the money was for me to look for and obtain a copy of my grandfather's birth certificate but they said that had nothing to do with them. So I left, knowing that I must live on the little money I had and report to immigration every six months while I'm here.

We arrived in Birmingham late in the evening. Even finding a taxi was a difficult thing to do, pushing our way through the crowds of people and dealing with everything that was so unfamiliar. But with the help of a very kind person, who directed us right to the taxi rank, we managed. We were very grateful for this help as being put into these circumstances makes you appreciate whatever you receive. It was dark and snowing hard. We had never seen snow before, but it felt like we were standing in a refrigerator. I wasn't sure about where to go, so I had to think fast—for I knew that relatives were reluctant to help anyone under immigration control. We took a taxi to Solihull, which cost me over twelve pounds, to a relative's place. We drove round and round trying to find the correct house but with no luck. We stopped and I asked the driver to please wait so that I could look for the correct house but he got cross and just threw us out with our bags. He even threatened to call the police if I didn't give him his money straight away. I tried pleading with him to help us and take us to the police station but he drove off at high speed and I felt that even if we had been able to chase after him he might well have run us over. He left us cold beyond belief and covered in snow. We couldn't go anywhere as carrying our suitcases was impossible. I didn't know what to do so we just stood on the side of the road looking around. There was nobody in sight because now it was going on midnight and I just started crying, holding my daughter and trying to protect ourselves from the snow with our hands. I began to imagine people finding us in the morning, a mother and daughter, asylum seekers, covered in snow and dead in the street. This was the worst time of my life. The year I will never forget—2001.

We were about to drop with the cold when, about an hour later, a car pulled up next to us and a young lady got out and as she got closer she could see that we were shaking from the cold and that something was terribly wrong. She asked us if we were lost. I could hardly speak for crying and my face felt frozen rigid. She shouted at the top of her voice for her boyfriend to come and help us and they guided us, one by one, into their car. After sitting for a short while in the warmth of their car, I managed to tell her that we were looking for a certain relative and by some miracle she knew who I was talking about and also the place were they stayed. Straight away she shouted to her boyfriend who helped us to carry our bags, because we could no longer hold anything. We even struggled to walk properly but luckily the place was only a few doors away—I had made a mistake with the house number. Yet again God had sent an angel to help me.

We went into my cousin's house but she wasn't there—she was working in London and only her sons were at home. They offered us a single bed to share for the night and luckily it was right by the hot water tank and we were lovely and warm. The following two days we were given only cups of tea. We assumed they didn't eat much or were short of food but I saw plenty of tinned beans and other goods in their food cupboards—but I didn't feel I could say anything. When my cousin rang from London she spoke only with her sons and when I asked to speak to her they just cut the call short and hung up. We only stayed there for about three days because I could sense that things were very awkward. We were an inconvenience. So I decided we should leave and we caught the bus—it was the first time we had seen a big double-decker—into Birmingham with no idea where we were going to stay. As we trundled along on the bus, we marvelled at the traffic and the beautiful buildings that Britain had. We just sat there until the bus driver told us where to get off and what to do. It was like he knew we were asylum seekers. Maybe, with all the humiliations we had to go through, we were easy to spot. After we had found some food and drink to keep us going in our search for freedom and sanctuary, we sat at the bus station in town, eating our egg sandwiches. We washed these down with water from the tap in the toilet but this made me so sick that I had to vomit all my food, which made me think that I had wasted my money. We sat on the bench watching all the people passing by. None of these people looked English—they all looked foreign, like refugees. That is when the idea came to me of finding the refugee council, who might help us.

We eventually found the Midland Refugee Council in Digbeth. We were interviewed by a young man called James—one of the nicest people I had met here in Britain. When I told him our story, we were made to wait while they sorted things out. After a couple of hours, when I was just starting to worry that it was getting dark and we would have nowhere to stay, we were given a taxi voucher and an address. Our journey wasn't over when we arrived at this address. A young Asian-looking gentleman then took us in his own car to an area called Ladywood. This would be our new accommodation until the authorities sorted out our paperwork.

When this young man opened the door to our accommodation and switched on the lights it was like looking into heaven. The place was filled with a warmth I could never explain. There was everything a woman could want to make a home—a fridge, stove, television, furniture and fitted carpets—even some groceries (some of the food we didn't even recognise) and it was just too beautiful for me. I can't explain how I felt at this point—this was home. That night we didn't eat or bathe—we just climbed into one of the double beds together, tucked under the thickest white duvets we'd ever seen and sank into a comfortable, dreamless sleep.

In the morning I rushed downstairs, scared that all that I had seen the night before had just been a dream. But no, all the furniture and groceries were still there and the snow was still outside. For me, there was nothing bad anybody could say about the British people's Government. They are very fair and good to the asylum seekers who enter Britain. Without all this help I think we would have come close to death.

The next few days went well but they turned into weeks. We just sat at home, not allowed to work and I decided to fight my case for vouchers because I was not getting any at this point because of the money they had found on me the first time I arrived.

When my second case appeal came up I had to look for a new solicitor. When asked at the hearing which country I had come from she didn't know, not even my name, so the case was dismissed. Waiting for my third appeal was tougher for me. All I felt as I stood in front of the Judge at this appeal was scared and afraid so I did more crying than talking and I know that I did not express myself well. I was afraid of the white man mostly, so I lost my case again. This time it felt like I was in a box, like I was suffocating.

My case for the appeal for vouchers had to go all the way to the Immigration Office at Croydon. I prayed all the way and kept myself fasting so that I lost weight. We were given an approval after a very long interrogation. They wanted to know from me how I spent my last thirty pounds. I couldn't help crying as I told the officer that I was buying a lot of pads because I had developed a bladder problem and had to change continuously. The shame of saying all this made my whole body weak. I could even feel my legs and hands shaking. I was then told to sit outside and in a few minutes was called back in and it was approved that I should go on to the voucher system.

At this time my two youngest children—Rosie and Christopher were still living in Zimbabwe with my husband. They were suffering—they lived on dried fish, beans and mostly green vegetables. My husband had no job and my son, Shane, was out of work too as most firms had closed down. The country was in a really bad situation. There was very little food and what was available would be very expensive or sold on the black market. The children were no longer going to school because there wasn't any money plus they were having racial problems with the teachers and some of the pupils. Things were becoming nasty. All this was because they were white and mixed race.

With all this happening in my life my health suffered. I started to get severe migraine headaches and sometimes I was rushed to hospital and I also started seeing the doctor because I couldn't stop crying—day and night. They put me on some tablets for my depression and this made life a little easier. This is when I started seeing the psychiatrist at the Hallam Street Hospital in West Bromwich for mental health problems. At night I got absolutely no sleep at all. It was like my brain refused to shut off—the problems just got worse and worse in my head. At times I could not climb my stairs, I had to crawl up on my hand and knees. My diarrhoea was so bad that I just stayed in the toilet and I had to wear incontinence pads all the time because I couldn't control my bladder.

My daughter Nippy met a man called John who she fell in love with. This was her first boyfriend and he was twenty-three years her senior. I tried to stop her but she refused, saying that her older brother had told her that she should get married to an older man and she would be his sweetheart. I put her on contraception but she didn't take them and was about two months pregnant when I found out. They then said they wanted to get married. I tried my best to make them wait but both of them wanted it that way so I just had to keep quiet.

In the middle of all this ill health and my sadness for my daughter, there was one bright point. We managed to collect enough money from well-wishers and friends all over the world to pay the air fare for Rosie and Christopher to come to Britain. When they arrived I was so happy to see them but they didn't recognize me. I had to shout their names out loud to get their attention. In the six months since I had left Zimbabwe I had grown older-looking and got fatter, with big bags under my eyes and brown patches on my face. This was such a happy moment in my life, having my other two children here with me at long last, where there would be some good healthy food and they could finish their schooling.

Christopher after his arrival in Britain

My daughter's wedding was a total mess. Firstly, John was late for the ceremony at the registry office and, secondly, he was so drunk at the reception that he took off all his clothes, showing everyone his private parts, even my young children. In shock and disgust we left for home.

A month after the wedding my daughter went to see a doctor for a check-up and when they took a scan they found out that she had developed lumps in her uterus. These were tested and found to be cancer, so she would have to be operated on and given a Caesarean birth because the lumps were blocking the passageway. When she told her husband this he didn't even look like he cared—he just went out and had a drink. Over the next week we found out that he was going to court for the custody of his three children from his previous girlfriend who had recently died. His children had been taken away by social services, so this is why he married my daughter. The marriage he had with my daughter was for his convenience, thinking he was going to win his case and would have a nice quiet woman who would never complain to look after his children. This was the first time my daughter had heard about the children or the girlfriend who had died. She also heard that he had divorced his previous wife two weeks before their wedding. All this was a shock to us all. He lost his case and then became very cruel because the mother of his children had passed away and he set himself to make my daughter suffer for his pain. Married life for her became a nightmare. Her husband drank on a daily basis. Even though it was winter there was no central heating of any kind and no hot water. The big bath was cracked, so he bathed in a small basin but he gave her a small bucket to wash in. He said this was OK because she came from Africa. A dog owned by John, called Penny, was kept in the bathroom and was not housetrained so it used the floor and my daughter was forced to clean the dog's mess. Whenever the dog went out in the night she had to go out and look for it because it was on heat. All the carpets in the house were all messed up with dog hairs but there was no broom or vacuum cleaner to help her to keep the place clean and the whole place smelled of dog shit. John and his son from his previous marriage, who lived with him, slept on two small chairs before the wedding—he only bought a bed at the time he got married. Things were so bad for Nippy—they lived on bread and baked beans because all the money they had went on 'White Lightning', a very strong and cheap cider sold in three litre bottles. He never once took into consideration that she was pregnant and had also been diagnosed with cancer. On occasion he used to smack her and call her all sorts of names, saying that she was going to give birth to a black monkey with a double barrel nose and he would spit at her. One night he repeated all this sort of thing but this time he put her in the toilet and flushed the chain. He hit her, and then said he wanted to stab her. She got away from him but she was in fear of her life and the next day she came home without him knowing. She also told me about the time when he choked her till she stopped breathing; she had a blackout and fell to the floor with her nose bleeding and she was coughing up blood.

When he came to the house a few days later, very drunk, kicking and shouting, I phoned the police. This is something I should have done long ago because my poor, sweet daughter's face was badly bruised by a man old enough to be her father; but when you are an asylum seeker you don't want to get into any involvements with the police for fear of being deported.

A few days later I woke up one morning feeling very depressed. I just sat on the bed crying uncontrollably. My son, Christopher, had just left for high school and my daughter Rosie had also left for college, saying goodbye as usual, without showing any signs that she was sick. I then asked my pregnant daughter, Nippy, to take me to the doctor at our local clinic, thinking maybe he could give me something to make me feel better. We sat down in the waiting room and watched as some nurses walked in with a stretcher. Before long my name was called to see a doctor. There were about twelve doctors on duty that day but I was called into the same room out of which a stretcher had just come. The doctor asked my name and when I told him he replied, 'Your young daughter, Rosie, is about to give birth—any minute now.' I got such a shock I started screaming to Jesus why all this was happening to me. I had no idea she was also pregnant and according to Nippy, who was sitting in the waiting room, all the people were so shocked hearing me crying out so loud, they thought the doctor might have cut my head off or something. The doctor was very kind. He had to give me a lot of counselling to get me through that experience. He was the best doctor I have ever known and is still my doctor to this day.

My caseworker was notified of all this going on in my life. She was a very nice young lady, who worked for the refugee council and took a lot of problems from us; you could see that she was very genuine—someone who really cared. She too got such a shock that Rosie was having a baby because there was nothing noticeable about her—absolutely no stomach. She rushed me straight to the hospital where I was just in time to witness the birth of the most beautiful baby with large blue eyes that were wide open, as though she were greeting me, saying, 'Hello Nana!' In an instant love just ran through my whole body and all I could do was cry with joy and love. This was my granddaughter, Kylie, who was born in October 2001.

My depression didn't get any better. Rosie and I had to take it in turns to look after Kylie at night because she was up every hour or so and then just drank a little and cried a lot. During this time I ate a lot and went from fourteen stone to over twenty stone. After a while things got so bad I couldn't climb the stairs—my weight was now such a problem. All this was because I was so afraid for my children and myself to be deported back to Zimbabwe, because I knew without doubt that if I had to go back I was going to be persecuted. All those war veterans causing trouble were my husband's friends and they knew me so well. Having been in Britain seeking asylum I was a marked woman and also I worked with the public for most of my life so many people knew me.

While all this was happening I had no idea my husband back in Zimbabwe was now married to a young girl from high school and had started up his own family. They were actually living together and had a child that was almost a year old. This new wife's parents were war veterans who my husband used to work with at Thornhill air force base in Gweru. When I contacted him with this story he just said that it was none of my business. At first I was very hurt because he was still my husband and I was fighting for a better life, thinking that one day he would follow me to Britain. He knew that I had had to leave first because both my grandfathers were white British, so we had both thought things were going to work out soon. Sadly, he showed me he couldn't wait. However, I think I am not the one who lost in all this as he gave up a good, faithful, hardworking woman for someone young enough to be his daughter. He also threatened me, saying that if I tried to claim any of the properties or monies that I had left behind with him, he would report me to the Zimbabwean immigration authorities and see a solicitor to say that I had kidnapped his son—and that I would have to pay him money. I think if I was not seeing a psychiatrist and taking something for my depression I would be locked away in a mental home by now.

It was time now for my daughter with cancer, Nippy, to give birth by Caesarean section. This was a happy and sad day. All this was so worrying and depressing to one's brain. Anyway, all went well—she gave birth to a handsome big baby of eight pounds five ounces. He was so white that you would never be able to tell that he was of mixed race. Of course, he had no double-barrelled nose or the looks of a black monkey, like all the ugly things Nippy's husband had said! How good things would have been if we all could share this wonderful feeling of special love. I am so sad that he never got to see his son, who looked the spitting image of his father. Some time later the same doctors took a scan and found that all the cancerous lumps had disappeared and they agreed with me that this must be some miracle. My grandson, Liam, was born in February 2002.

16

Still Waiting but Glad to be Here

One thing that really helped change my life was when my sister-in-law Lynette—a born-again Christian who lives in London—contacted me by telephone. Our main conversation was about Jesus and how he can help you in times of hardship and need. It was not long after that she and Pastor Phyllis visited me in Birmingham. We had a big family meeting and we all prayed and discussed the Bible. When they returned to London I still carried on with my Bible reading and almost daily I would receive a call from Lynette who became such an inspiration to me and a wonderful friendship blossomed. This made me see my life more and more clearly and every day I began to read my Bible, taking Jesus seriously again into my life. I was baptized into the Pentecostal church at Great Yarmouth in 2003. If Jesus had been in my heart when I came to Britain, I'm sure I would have been a much stronger person and would have been able to express all my feelings to the immigration officials at my hearings.

I still have my depression but the psychiatrist has really helped. One ailment that I experienced in my first year or two here was that my toenails started to curl inwards and they eventually became so small that they were digging into my feet, and I could not wear shoes for long. The reason I did not see a chiropodist was that I thought the nails would have to be removed, but, as my depression got better, my nails returned to their normal condition and it showed me that there are really some things that we will never understand about the human body.

I have had a series of solicitors to help—or hinder me—in my fight to stay in Britain. The first ones, as I have said, did not even remember my name or where I had come from so the case was dismissed without a proper hearing. My second solicitors were also from Birmingham and my appeal handled by them got another refusal. I did not feel that they tried hard enough with all the information available to them. I know I played my part in the failure of this appeal—the magistrate must have thought I was some sort of crazy person as I stood and cried before him, almost unable to speak. My father always called me 'weeping willow' because I could never fight hard without breaking down in tears.

After losing these appeals I felt desperate and started to scout around for someone to help me through the maze—someone like an immigration consultant. I met a lady who had been fighting her case for eight years but who had been helped by such a person and she introduced me to him. On the day of the appointment I went into his office and he asked my daughter Jane who accompanied me, to take a seat while leading me to another office. He explained to me that he had helped plenty of women like me but that you had to be nice to him first. He asked me about my ancestral rights and I gave him by parents' birth certificates. After filing these away, he opened a drawer and pulled out a condom, which he placed on the desk between us. He said I must be a very lonely woman without a man in my life and that if I listened to him I would have lots of favours and I would definitely be granted my stay in this country. I got such a shock. I thought that someone who dealt with legal matters like this should not even think of behaving like this and I got out of his office as fast as I could, crying as I went and leaving all my certificates there.

My next solicitor was recommended to me by my cousin, Nazarene, who came to Britain the year before me. She got her stay granted at her first appeal and told me that I had the wrong solicitors. I then consulted her solicitors in Bradford but found the constant travelling between Birmingham and Bradford very stressful. This was not helped by my depressed state and the diarrhoea and incontinence that I suffered from. One Sunday morning I woke up crying after having one of my nightmares and the phone was ringing. It was my solicitor and my hands started to shake and the tears flowed down my face, as I feared this was the news I dreaded—deportation.

But it was good news. He told me that the children and I had got our stay. Suddenly all the tears stopped and I thanked him before telling him I would have to phone him back. I couldn't wait one second longer to tell my children this wonderful news. As I shouted up the stairs for them they came running, wondering what could possibly be causing this excitement. We were soon hugging and kissing and talking—everyone at once—about our plans. I can't begin to explain the excitement. We were happy at last, thinking we had the greatest gift of all—our freedom—and that the children would at last stop getting persecuted by other children for being asylum seekers. After half an hour or more the phone rang again. I greeted my solicitor with a bright, happy voice but everything was to change as he told me that he had read the report incorrectly—we had been short by just two months on the amnesty that was required to get our stay. I put the phone down, choking on my tears, and the children guessed what had happened. All the happiness we had felt only a few moments before evaporated into thin air.

A few days later this same solicitor called again and asked me to go to Bradford to complete some forms on ancestral rights. He was very optimistic that we would get our stay in this way as many of my family members had used exactly the same paperwork and details. My bad luck with solicitors continued when I phoned to check on the progress of this process and heard a message on the answering machine saying that the firm had closed down. There was no way of contacting this solicitor to get my file from him. I even went to the offices in Bradford but they were locked up and deserted. I tried my local M.P. but he couldn't help me so I ended up at the Citizens Advice Bureau who advised me to get in touch with the Law Society. They managed to trace my files in Leeds and they were sent to my home so I was on the search for yet another solicitor. I got a list from my M.P. and am now with a firm in Birmingham that is treating me very well. I deal with a young Muslim lady called Aisha, who is one of the most understanding people I have ever met—yet another angel directed to help me.

My application for ancestral rights is pending and I'm carrying on the fight, reporting weekly to the immigration in Solihull. It's a frustrating process but I live in hope. What hurts the most is that most of my relatives from Zimbabwe are being given their stay on ancestral grounds with the right to work and do as they please with exactly the same documentation as I have—except that they applied in Zimbabwe. The solicitors I had were not very good and nothing much was done to help my case. With my new solicitors, here in Birmingham, I am positive that I will succeed in finally obtaining my stay. It is especially distressing to me that even some of the very dangerous people who we ran away from in Zimbabwe are being granted asylum. These are the war veterans who destroyed our lives and killed the white farmers.

Despite the comfort of my religion and the support I got from Lynette, I began to feel a very lonely woman, filling out and just getting older and older with each passing day. I decided to join a pen friend society and, after a few false starts, began to correspond with a man who understood all the suffering I was going through. With this friendship some of my depression has lifted but with my immigration status still unsettled it sometimes feels as though there are hands squeezing my head. Every now and again I break down into uncontrollable tears and I just have to run to my room, put my church music on and pray.

At the sweet age of 52 I have found true love again and got engaged in May 2005 to Ken, the Englishman of my dreams. He is similar in looks and ways to my grandfather whom I feel is looking down on me and smiling. I have made the right choice of man at long last. Ken has read this book several times and now I only have to mention Aida's name to him and his eyes will well up and the tears will come flooding down his face. My engagement ring is made up of three stones and because he still regards me as being 'married' to Aida he says the stones signify Aida, Ken and me. When I am granted my stay we shall get married.

After five years away I still miss the members of my family who have remained in Zimbabwe, but I am continuing my fight to stay here. I did, however, recently have the chance to see one member of my family—my sister Wendy, who had moved to South Africa. In time for Christmas 2005 she and her new husband Raymond paid a visit to the UK—the first time I had seen Wendy in seven years and the first time I had met Raymond in nearly forty years as he had been a friend of mine in high school. The weeks before her visit were agony. Wendy was like the only real friend I had ever had—we had done everything together in our young days, in the words of the Lulu song, 'from crayon to perfume', and I could hardly sleep or think of anything else at all. But when she arrived at my front door, I felt happier than ever before and could hardly stop kissing her. It was only when we fell in a heap into the shoe rack that I keep in my hallway that we stopped kissing and started laughing and talking.

Sharing all the memories of our childhood, schooldays and family, we never stopped talking all during her visit. This was all so wonderful that it made me wonder who I would laugh and share my stories with when she returned to South Africa. This was something I could only do with my sister. I had not planned to go to the airport to see off Wendy and Raymond, as I had the feeling it would be the last time I would see them—as has been the case with everybody else in my life to whom I have said goodbye. The night before they were due to depart I decided to go with them to the airport, after my fiancé Ken arranged time off work to accompany me.

The alarm went off at 2.30 a.m. as the taxi had been booked for 3.30 a.m. to take all four of us to Birmingham airport. To my surprise, on the journey I did not cry but simply felt empty and sad. All the fun and laughter was coming to an end. After they had checked in we all went for a coffee and then it was time for us all to say our farewells. As they made their way up the automatic stairs to the departure lounge I had to choke back my tears as I waved them goodbye. If my fiancé had not been there to support and comfort me, I think I would have run up those stairs and cried for her to return, if not for another day but just to kiss and cuddle her one last time.

I had a fantastic Christmas with my sister and it brought back memories of the family with whom we had lost touch because we're spread through so many countries. There is my brother Robin who qualified as a doctor in Florida. We are so proud of him but he does not keep in contact. It is eleven years now since we saw or heard from him. Throughout that Christmas my thoughts would continually stray to the family I had left behind in Zimbabwe. They would spend most of Christmas sleeping because there is no food for them. The situation gets more and more desperate in Zimbabwe and I worry about them constantly but feel helpless.

My brother Robin (left)

The 'Seal' family:
Mummy seal, daddy seal and baby seal—according to Liam (Me, Ken and Liam)

My fiancé is a lovely man. The first time he stayed overnight in my home rather than going to his own, which was two bus rides away, he brought me breakfast in bed. As he put on the light, I saw him standing there with a tray containing toast and apricot jam, a cup of tea and some juice plus a card and a little cuddly monkey. He wished me 'Happy Valentine's Day' and announced that he had booked the day off work to be with me. I was so happy! This was our second Valentine's together and he was the first person to spoil me in a very long time. Feeling loved and actually belonging to someone so special made me hungry for the wonderful meal on the tray. This feeling of happiness was soon tinged with sadness when I realised it was 14th February 2006. I had now been in Britain a full five years and was still waiting for the immigration authorities to make a decision on my case. It was also my brother Harold's fiftieth birthday and it would be the fifth birthday that we hadn't been able to share. I couldn't hold back my sadness.

During the five years since I arrived with Nippy, my family has grown and thrived. My oldest son Shane is one of the loveliest young men I have ever met. He left Zimbabwe shortly after Rosie and Christopher had joined me in Britain.

With the help of family members, he emigrated to New Zealand with his wife Kay, his daughter and two sons. His daughter Dehandra is the spitting image of my little Aida. This was like some miracle that Jesus made. Shane works full time as a technician and is also a preacher at the local Pentecostal church. He is now very happy as he has been granted citizenship of New Zealand and would love me to join him there one day. It is always a grandmother's dream to watch her grandchildren growing up but as I have got grandchildren born here in Britain, I would only be able to visit New Zealand for a holiday to see them all. Shane telephones me every week and tells me all that he and his family are doing and how much he loves me.

My four grandchildren in Britain
L-R: Daniel, Liam, Kylie and Kyle

Kylie and Liam

My second daughter, Jane (Nippy), obtained a divorce from John shortly after Liam was born. She met her second husband Anton in July 2004 and they got married in the November. All my life I had always wanted to ride in a limousine and Anton hired one to take me from my home to their wedding at the registry office at West Bromwich and from there to the reception. I even had champagne to drink while travelling. Anton is the exact opposite of John; he is loving, kind and generous and treats my daughter like a queen and is also a very good son-in-law to me. My only regret is that Nippy has changed from being a naughty, talkative girl to being a very quiet, shy person, all because when my other daughter, Aida, was so ill I left Nippy with a friend who was mostly at work and an auntie who abused my child by hitting her all the time and there was nobody that noticed all this. But she is so sweet and gentle that you can't help but love her and I try to make up to her for all the times I had not been there for her. In August 2005, after a lot of medical problems, Nippy gave birth by Caesarean section, three weeks before her due date, to a baby boy weighing nearly nine pounds. They have named him Daniel. He has a full mop of black hair, wide-open, big, brown eyes and he looks like a little Eskimo. On his right-hand little finger he has three distinct creases rather than the usual two. This is a family trait from my mother's side of the family. My grandfather Jimmy, my mother, myself and one of Shane's sons also have this. It can be on the left or right-hand little finger.

Jane on her wedding day to Anton

My third daughter Rosie is someone who reminds me so much of my younger self; we are like two sides of the same coin. She has only one problem though—she blames me for whatever goes wrong and is not thankful for anything the family does for her. She just takes it for granted that it is my duty and that we are below her standard. What she does not realize is that one day she will be sorry because life is too short and we have to love each other and make the most of it. We should not wish for a better family than the one Jesus has given us. She is the only child that has tormented me and blames me for her being an asylum seeker. If anything should go wrong with her future decisions I will always love her and be there for her. In July 2005 she gave birth to a baby boy of six pounds five ounces by her long-term partner Kristian. Baby Kyle has the most beautiful blue eyes that look like some sort of gemstones. They have named him Kyle Ebenezer. This has made me very proud as they named him Ebenezer after my paternal grandfather. Rosie may have her faults, but, like my mother said about me, I would vote her the 'best mother in the world'.

My last-born son, Christopher, is not anything like his father. He is a very considerate young man who loves his mother and his family. He left high school last year and is now doing AS level courses at Dudley College. During the summer break he had to sit at home each day instead of going out with his friends or going on holiday. He would have loved a summer job to earn some pocket money for himself but he is not allowed to work. If given the chance he wants to become a doctor. He is always consulting a copy of the Home Emergency Guide to diagnose the symptoms of all the illnesses I have suffered whilst here in Britain. Some of his artwork from school was selected to be exhibited at the Wednesbury Art Gallery and Museum, which made me feel so proud and happy. I always wanted him to be the best as people have negative views about asylum seekers.

Christopher with his artwork displayed in Wednesbury Art Gallery

Christopher on being awarded his GCSE certificates

My father is now an old man and still lives in South Africa with my sister Wendy. He did until recently live in Gweru, mining gold, but he was forced to leave after his home was set alight by unknown persons and he suffered burns and was hospitalised for a week. I have not seen my father since I left Zimbabwe. I feel like a little girl who still wants her Daddy, to sit on his lap, cry to him and tell him all her sorrows. I still miss my mother and think of her often. As far back as I can remember when I lived with my parents, my mother played Charley Pride's records (an African-American country music singer) and would often shed a tear as she listened. She never explained to us why she was crying, but simply said that he was a good country and western singer who made every word he sang so much better than life itself. My mother bought every one of Charley Pride's records, as did her sisters, who enjoyed the same music. Having listened every day when I was young to his music I now consider it traditional music and buy all his releases myself. Every time there was some sort of occasion, Charley Pride records were played. My only comfort when I came to Britain was the Charley Pride CDs that my son, Christopher, bought me and I treasure them with my life. Christopher knew I loved this music and had walked to school (it was an hour's walk and he often had sore feet), saving his bus fares to buy me a 3 CD boxed set. I play them on a daily basis. I feel the same love for this music as my mother did—he is a man who sings of true happenings, of things so real and I hope one day to meet him in person and not just in my dreams.

We are happy here in Britain in the house provided to my family by Sandwell Council. This year, for the first time in years, I have planted some flowers and vegetables and have also redecorated. I had got into trouble for tearing off the old wallpaper as the design had broad stripes, which reminded me of the prison bars in Oakington. Even if things don't work out the way I planned, I honestly think that all the suffering I have endured since coming to Britain has been worth it, seeing as my family has doubled. I will never give up on my goal of living in Britain—both my grandfathers were white British and this is where I belong. I have hope for the future because I have my grandchildren who were born here. And today I thank my Jesus that I do have a wonderful man who understands me and one day intends to marry me.

My happiness is tinged by sadness whenever I hear about the situation back in Zimbabwe. The country is in crisis and my family back there live on wild meat with just salt and water and are barely surviving. My sister-in-law told me of one horrendous incident when my brother Graham—the fifth in the family—got into a tussle with some people who were trying to steal from him. The thief bit off one of his fingers during the fight and swallowed it! As if this weren't bad enough, they are now struggling to pay the hospital bill for his treatment. I live in fear of the day when I get even worse news—that one of my family has been killed or starved to death.

Once again Immigration is shifting us for the fourth time since here in Britain and this is so upsetting for my family.

I hope the people who read my book, which is a true story, will start believing in caring for one another and not think that everyone who seeks asylum is bad. Seeking asylum is a big move. It means starting again from the beginning and escaping from a bad life. I do not think that people in their right minds would leave the country they were born in to come all this way only to be refused entry unless they were desperate. Right now I feel I am in limbo, as Britain does not want me and I feel as though I never belonged in Zimbabwe because of all the abuse I suffered in its many different forms. All I want to do now is live a happy life and watch my family grow old and when it is time for me to die, I want to be buried where I belong—in Britain. One more thing I would say—a lady of my age would have never left for another country to seek asylum without very good reasons.

GOD BLESS

End

Me and Wendy—Christmas 2005

Me—Christmas 2005

Epilogue

Below is the latter Aida wrote on the day before she died:

24-8-87

Dear Mummy

How are you all doing? I'm trying to get better. The doctors are all going to have a meeting about me tomorrow. Can you give Beryl, Sonya and the other friends the hospital's address so that they can write me a letter. Aunty Wendy did not come today or 'phone at all. I am missing you all and hope you can come soon.

Lots of love

Aida

See Appendix A for an extract from a letter by the doctor in charge of Aida prior to her death on the 25th August 1987.

APPENDIX A

DATE: 20 June 2002

TO WHOM IT MAY CONCERN

This is to certify that I was the doctor in charge of Aida Jenkins (dob 16/2/73) from 16 June 1987 until her death on 25 August 1987 in Ward 285 of the Johannesburg Hospital, South Africa.

She had been transferred from Zimbabwe with—

1. Chronic renal failure on peritoneal dialysis, (her serum creatinine was 262 mmol/l prior to her death). The cause of her renal failure was diffuse proliferative glomerulonephritis.
2. Congestive cardiac failure without hypertension, and this was thought to be due to cardiomyopathy.
3. Severe malnutrition.
4. Multiple contractures.
5. Bed sores.
6. Chronic diarrhea which responded to cholestyramine.

Despite careful hyperalimentation as well as enteral feeds including Portagen over the 2 months she was with us, she died on 25 August 1987. This was thought to be due to cardiac failure.

PETER D THOMPSON MBBCh FCP (SA)
Formerly Professor of Paediatric Nephrology
University of The Witwatersrand, Johannesburg
And presently Locum Consultant Paediatric Nephrology, St James's Hospital, Leeds

APPENDIX B

TO WHOM IT MAY CONCERN

I have come to know Mabel Honde (Pike) over the last year or so and can confirm her to be a responsible, pleasant and hard-working person. She is very much a family person and has children and grandchildren in the United Kingdom.

I first came into contact with Mabel when she asked me to help her with her autobiographical book *Cry With Me*. I have edited the book for her and have been truly horrified by the conditions in which she had to live in the last few years that she spent in Zimbabwe. Her life there was difficult at best and extremely dangerous at worst. I am unable to comprehend how people can cope with some of the things that have happened to her at the hands of what she refers to as 'war veterans' and officials.

I have no hesitation in vouching for her good character.

Bernice Walmsley

978-0-595-67874-7
0-595-67874-2

Printed in the United Kingdom
by Lightning Source UK Ltd.
114584UKS00002B/100-108

9 780595 678747